LIVING LIFE ON MY TERMS

The Inspiring Guide for Success and Happiness

Author: Daniel Skarie

Copyright © 2015 Daniel Skarie

Skarie Enterprises LLC
www.signstoinspire.com

Living Life On My Terms: The Inspiring Guide for Success and Happiness, Author Daniel Skarie, Published by Skarie Enterprises LLC. www.signstoinspire.com

Copyright 2015 by Daniel Skarie and Skarie Enterprises LLC All Rights Reserved. No part of this publication may be reproduced, stored in a retrieval system or transmitted in any form or by any means, electronic mechanical, photocopying, recording or otherwise, without the written permission of the publisher.

Skarie Enterprises LLC and its logo and Marks are trademarks of Skarie Enterprises LLC

Cover layout and design by Daniel Skarie and Trevor Skarie

Copyright © 2015 Daniel Skarie
Skarie Enterprises LLC
www.signstoinspire.com

Contents

- Dedication
- Introduction
- I. Challenges of Life
- II. Creating the Best Surroundings
- III. The Power of Positive Thinking
- IV. The 12 Key Elements for Success and Happiness
- V. Transforming Positive Thought to a Positive Life
- VI. Affirmations for Motivation and Success
- VII. Defining Goals for Success
- VIII. Formula for Success in Life
- IX. Personal Time and Meditation
- X. Reflections and Quotes to Live By

LIVING LIFE ON MY TERMS

The Inspiring Guide for Success and Happiness

Dedication

I dedicate this book to my family and God for giving me the inspiration to share my philosophy, knowledge, and strategies to the world to help people live the most enjoyable, rewarding, and successful life they can while pursuing inner peace and understanding to find true happiness and fulfillment in life, both personally and professionally. My wish is this book will inspire you to live the life you choose to live.

Daniel Skarie

Introduction

"We live our lives in this world by how we see it. Change your view from within and change the world."

This quote is so simple yet holds so much truth to life. It really isn't about what we have or who we are, but how we see things and what we do about it. We all want to live a life of happiness. We have goals, dreams, a vision of the life we want to live and the person we want to be, but life was never intended to be easy. It challenges us from every direction, knocking us down every chance it gets, but for every time we are knocked down we have a choice to stand again, dust ourselves off, and learn from our challenges so we can keep moving forward in life. It's human nature to want to learn and evolve and take on the challenges to grow as an individual. The question is how we can achieve what we want in life when it seems life has handed us nothing but obstacles.

Someone once asked me to define the meaning of life, and I said, "It's not about defining it, it's about living it. It's about the journey, and it's about the moments and challenges that will define life differently for each and every person." Life is about following your heart and dreams in pursuit of living a life with all the happiness and success that resides deep within you, no matter what happens.

Life is about challenges, it's about change, and it's about living to learn and learning to live. So the real question is, how does one live a life of happiness and success no matter what mistakes are made, and what hand was dealt to us in life? One of the keys to life is **"Happiness and enjoyment of life comes not from what** you have or don't have, but your perception of life itself and the moments that it brings you and what you do with those moments, and that is the definition of a champion."

The journey of the human spirit is a beautiful experience, but not an easy one, and if you're willing to live your life and not just survive it, you can see the beauty in even the darkest days of your life story. It's also discovering and evolving as a person to be as successful as you can in all aspects of your life, from your personal life to how you earn a living. Another key to life is discovering the meaning behind the challenges we face in pursuit of finding fulfillment and happiness in the lives we live to learn and grow as a person in the path we choose to take.

The first thing you must remind yourself is **"Happiness is not a place or thing, it's a state of mind."** By taking charge of your mind, your perspective, and your approach to life, it puts you in the driver's seat for where you want to go and how you get there.

"Life is not about finding yourself, it's about creating yourself."

Take a journey with me through the pages ahead as I reveal key secrets, strategies, and techniques for taking control of your life and how to reach new heights in your career, relationships, finances, self motivation, and drive to live an inspiring-filled life with all the success and happiness you seek. In this book, you'll also find my reflections on life as summaries of great thoughts of inspiration and meaning behind moments we all face in this wonderful life to help you achieve your life goals.

We all face different challenges in our life. For some, it's surviving some setbacks in life right now, or having financial problems, a weight problem, fighting an addiction, challenges with your love life or family, or overcoming a disease. Perhaps you've done well for yourself in business but still feel you're not reaching your full potential that lies within you and want to reach that next level of success. Maybe you've reached great success in business but at the cost of your family life. I believe this book will inspire and teach you the key elements to achieving what your heart desires to live the life you choose.

In the pages ahead, we will dive into the main components to reaching the greatest potential that lies within you. Here are some of the key things I'll share with you.

- How to view challenges in life as lessons to propel you to reaching new heights.
- To take charge of your surroundings and create the environment you want to live and work in, filled with inspiration, peace, motivation, and happiness.
- The 12 key elements for success and happiness for a positive and fulfilling life.
- How to discipline and train the human mind to focus and bring to reality what you want in life like success, ample wealth, inner peace, abundant love, you name it.
- One of the greatest focusing techniques used by some of the most successful people of all time, and how to apply it to your goals in life.
- Formula for success to turn dreams into reality.
- Techniques for reenergizing the body and soul, build focus, and clearing the mind for inner peace.
- How to take control of your life by becoming emotionally aware of yourself, your perception of life, and the deep meanings of life itself.

Chapter I
Challenges of Life

I. Challenges of Life

The great Muhammad Ali once said, "Champions aren't made in the gyms. Champions are made from something they have deep inside them - a desire, a dream, and a vision."

Success is not something that just happens, it's something you achieve when you pursue it against all odds and you're willing to overcome any obstacles to get there. You have to want it, you have to pursue it, and you need to keep moving forward no matter what to achieve it. I believe if you find the desire within yourself, you can become a champion in whatever you do or have a passion for in life. The key is to find the meaning behind your goals, dreams, or career.

I came across a saying once that stuck with me from a movie, "Your actions need meaning. If you're going to fight, you fight for a cause, a purpose, and it should be for something greater than yourself." What it means is we need to find the purpose and meaning behind our goals and actions. To find the strength to conquer our goals and what kind of difference it can make in ourselves and in the people around us. This becomes the fuel for our inspiration to prevail no matter what challenges lie ahead.

Many people live a life of physical and emotional exhaustion just trying to survive this world and the challenges they face. The key is it's the challenges in life that gives us our fuel for motivation. The individual that takes their challenges and uses them to propel themselves to succeed, or to make a difference in this world, is what can make a person great.

Life doesn't come easy, it's something we have to work at every day of our lives in pursuit of success and happiness, to live that perfect life we envision in our mind, whatever that may be. Life doesn't always play out the way we envision it, but if we change our perspective and approach on life, it can work out better then we envisioned with more success and happiness then we ever thought possible, if we can learn to enjoy the journey, the lessons, and the challenges along the way.

"You can't have triumph without struggles and it's within these struggles that we can find ourself, define ourself, and truly live."

"Life is about learning to live and living to learn."
Life is also about change, and what would life be like without our challenges that bring change? After all, it's our challenges that define us and make us who we are. Just look at nature and the animal kingdom. We are surrounded by stories of evolutionary change caused by its challenges. Over time, plants evolved to grow thorns to protect itself, or how about the gazelle gaining its speed to run away from the big cats of Africa. Without challenges, we don't have a reason for change.

Imagine being able to pick up a golf club for the first time and having a perfect swing and getting a hole in one with your first shot and every shot thereafter…would there be a point in picking up the sport as a hobby if there was no challenge in it? It's our human nature to challenge ourselves to become more than what we are and to keep evolving. Golf, as an example, has been defined as a great sport, like many others, because we are really playing against ourselves. It's a game that challenges us mentally, not just physically, as a team of one. But the real challenge is learning to master ourselves to get the body to perform what the mind wants us to accomplish. So we play the sport day after day trying to find the best within ourselves. This is also why you find the true greats of any sport had a true love for the game, and not just the pursuit of winning the game.

A wise man once said, "Life cannot be taught, it must be experienced to be understood to truly learn from it." I believe how we choose to embrace our challenges in life also determines how much we learn from them, good and bad.

We are not all athletes, but the same principals apply to life in general. Most people want to succeed in all aspects of their life, from their personal life to their professional life. But it's the challenges that make it worthwhile to learn and evolve, and most importantly, our perspective on life that truly determines if we are happy. That is the definition of success. If you can master this, then you will win no matter what the outcome is. Sometimes it's just that mental switch we need to find within ourselves to discover the right frame of mind we are all looking for, to feel at peace and be truly happy no matter what life brings our way.

Sometimes we just need to remind ourselves that **"Life is not about the destination it's about the journey."** If we can shift our way of thinking to be more concerned about **living in the moment** and absorbing as much life as we can from these moments and challenges, then we'll be successful within any component of our life.

Whether we admit it or not, we bring a lot of our pain and suffering on ourselves just by our perspective, but we don't have to. **"Happiness is not a cause, it's a choice."**

A person could argue there are many things in our life that we cannot change; we can't change our family members just because we're not getting along with our children, parents, or siblings. We can't change the fact that we need to work hard to earn a living to make it through this life to pay for the things we need, like a roof over our head and food on the table. We can't change the past, like the loss of a loved one, or a disease we had to face, but some things we can change. **"Everything is about choices,"** even if we're only talking about how we view a so-called problem in our life.

The human spirit is an amazing thing, but we allow ourselves to get dragged down with our challenges versus looking at them as gifts. We can easily forget not to give our problems and challenges credit for what they do give us. It's the challenges in our life that make us who we are, but how we choose to see the problem is what sets the tone for what we get out of the experience. If we can learn to view our problems and challenges as gifts of opportunity to learn and experience life from, then we can learn and evolve as a person far more. Then you're really living life, not just surviving life, and isn't that what we really want?

I've known two women close to me that have survived breast cancer and had two very different experiences from it. One of them allowed it to drag her down with depression and sorrow, and the other chose to keep working and not allow the cancer to affect her daily view on life and took on each day with a smile, refusing to allow the cancer (no matter what the outcome would be) to affect the things that brought her joy in her life.

If you were given the news today that you had 6 months or less to live, you still have a choice to fight or give up. Do you choose to swim in regret, sorrow, and anger, or do you hold your head up high and live your last few months on earth embracing what time you have left with love for life and for your family and friends you have around you.
"You control your life, life does not control you."

No matter what country you live in, rich or poor, everyone is surrounded by the challenges of life, big and small. And a person can easily find themselves at the receiving end of what seems to be an endless amount of negative emotions; like pain, frustration, sorrow, anger, hate, you name it. Everybody has a story, but I'm here to remind you that you don't have to be the victim of all the negative emotions life can bring at you. We are also surrounded by stories of individuals that prove this to us. We have all heard amazing stories of miracles or amazing triumphs of an individual overcoming their life challenges. Struggles like the battle against a terminal disease or surviving against all odds. But the truth is we all have it within ourselves to make the same choice in how we live our lives.

Personal Life Challenge

I've had to face a very serious challenge myself. When I was a small child I was diagnosed with a severe case of asthma. It started at the age of 2 when I was showing signs of breathing problems, including coming down with a very severe case of bronchitis. At the age of 4, my breathing and respiratory problems were finally diagnosed as a serious case of asthma. In the years to follow, I faced a very challenging childhood with breathing problems and many trips to the hospital.

Even today, I can remember back to when I was 4 and the vacation of a lifetime that went horribly wrong. My parents decided to take me and my 2 sisters on a wonderful vacation to Disney World. Little did they know that I would become dangerously ill with asthma on our trip. A few days into the trip I became very sick with serious problems breathing and had to be rushed to the hospital with the ER doing everything they could to stabilize my breathing. At the time, nebulizer breathing treatments were very new and we didn't have them in the Minnesota hospitals where we lived, but luckily they did have them in Florida. I reached a point where the hospital was even considering giving me a tracheotomy if the nebulizer treatments failed, for fear of respiratory failure. The good news is the breathing treatments worked and put me on the road to recovery. The cause of my breathing problems on our vacation was asthma brought on by the air conditioning system in the hotel with strong levels of mold, and high levels of chlorine in the pool, which I spent a lot of time playing in.

To this day, I still remember this trip with great detail even at such a young age because it was so traumatic, and let me tell you it's a terrifying feeling to struggle to breathe and with no end of relief in sight. It's like slowly suffocating for hours on end with nothing to reach for. Your body aches in pain as the muscles around the chest and back tire with exhaustion and overuse from hours of struggling to breathe. You find yourself focusing on each breath hoping for a little relief each time, and your next breath is all you can think about.

One positive thing I do remember about the situation and from the stories my family still tells of this trip, is of my mother. She was determined to take care of the situation and was already showing me at a young age that no matter how serious the problem, we can handle it. There was no panicking, no fear shown, and no tears from my parents, only the determined love to take care of me and the situation and make me smile again. As you can imagine, I did recover from this, otherwise I would not be here to write this today, but this was the beginning to a very long childhood of challenges with asthma.

As the years went on, I had my ups and downs with doctors trying to find the newest and ideal medication to keep my asthma under control, but if I came down with even a cold it would affect my breathing and spike my asthma out of control and I would find myself in the hospital. Between the ages of 4 and 12, I was in the ER regularly, sometimes twice a month. But no matter how seriously sick I may have gotten, my mother's determination and love for me with how she emotionally handled the situation gave me strength to always push on and beat it. She would always know just the right thing to say to make me feel at ease and taught me to not become lost in the problem, but focus on the solution and I would get better. Since my mother never showed me her fear, it gave me courage to never give up. I would be lying if I said none of us had fear, but we can choose what emotions we are going to focus on, and I believe that makes a difference on the outcome.

When my asthma acted up, there were many nights that I would have to sleep sitting up while struggling to breathe, focusing on each breath trying to get enough oxygen in my body. My muscles would ache in pain from overuse trying to breathe for hours and hours with little help from medication. I reached a point a few times that I told my mother, "Just let me die, I can't do this any longer, I can't breathe," as I sit up in bed ready to pass out from exhaustion. What could be more challenging than hearing your own child asking for death for relief? She always showed me strength and went with the mindset that everything will work out but we can't give up, and to focus on what we can do to make this better. Easy for her to say, since I'm the one running low on willpower after fighting the same fight so many nights and over so many years, but with every battle won, more courage was born. Over the years I never gave up, and I gave it 110% on working through my asthma problems.

When I was 7, I remember having a bad enough episode of asthma that it caused a collapsed lung and I spent 3-4 days in the hospital. I still remember to this day the doctors telling us that I would spend a few days in the hospital while they would do around-the-clock nebulizer treatments and lung massages to help the lungs and see if the lung would re-inflate by itself. If not, then they would have to insert a needle in my side to manually inflate it. Well that became my goal; I would inflate my own lung back up. The doctors and nurses were amazed over the strength and positive attitude I had for the situation. Typically a child of my age would be in a great deal of chest and back pain and have very little interest in moving around and playing. I chose not to let this stop me and had every intention of getting better and not letting this slow me down. I even spent time cheering up some other kids staying at the hospital with my talking puppet I brought from home. In the end, I was able to inflate my own lung without help from the doctors.

As a young child, I was already realizing it's all about choices and how we look at a problem. When I reached the age of 10, I learned my limitations with asthma and the right medications to keep it under control as best we could, but I pushed it to the limit almost daily because I loved sports and refused to let the disease own me and stop me from what I wanted to do.

By the time I was 12, I was known among all my friends and classmates as incredibly fast and athletic, despite my asthma creating barriers as to how far I could push myself athletically.

Learning determination and motivation from my mother, I refused to allow my asthma to stop me from doing what I wanted to do, including playing sports. Playing team sports was very challenging with my asthma, but with my friends I did it all and was exceptionally good at it. By the age of 13, I fell in love with weight lifting. Weight lifting had little impact on my breathing but I could build on my physical strength and it turned out to have a large impact on my lungs and asthma overall. With weight lifting and improvements in medicine, I now have very little trouble keeping my asthma at bay, but I will never forget all those long nights reaching a point of exhaustion from struggling to breathe and having to make a choice; to roll over and cry or stand tall and focus on the positive that I can beat this, I will beat this, and I will not allow the disease to control me, I will control the disease.

There are plenty of far more difficult life stories out there of people overcoming a serious physical or medical challenge then mine, but my point is this; how we choose to embrace our challenges can make a serious impact on the overall outcome of the results and will shape the very person you are and who you become.

Fighting to Live

Here is another personal life story that's a great example of determination and controlling one's perspective on a problem. My father has passed away, but my mother has remarried to a great guy, Paul. A few years into their marriage, Paul was diagnosed with a serious medical problem that would prove to be his greatest challenge in life and also created an everlasting impression on how he would view life, and live life, from that point on.

In the summer of 2004, Paul was rushed to the hospital for intense pain in the abdomen. It was discovered that the gallbladder had completely ruptured and there was very little left of it, causing septicemia (poisoning internally from the fluid). This wasn't the really bad news. Over the past couple of years, doctors had already been monitoring a liver problem from an unknown cause, but now his liver was officially failing.

Paul was now facing a ruptured gallbladder and a failing liver, and would require a liver transplant and removal of the gallbladder if he is to survive.

He was put on a waiting list for a liver transplant, but the gallbladder was also a serious problem. They could not operate to remove the gallbladder because his blood was to thin from the failing liver, so it would have to wait until the liver transplant, which made this a race against time. If you've ever known anyone that has gone through needing an organ transplant, the average person waits months to get to the top of the waiting list and find the ideal donor, and to get to the top of the list also means death is knocking at your door.

What does one do or say when faced with such a challenge that seems impossible to overcome, racing against time to stay alive long enough for modern medicine to replace what is now failing inside you? This is one of those moments in life when a person must choose....do you stand and fight or let fate decide the outcome. Do you choose to turn your cheek to life and all that's in it becoming angry and full of hate, sorrow, and depression, asking why me? Or do you choose to embrace life and everyone around you and say, "I will beat this or die trying," with a smile.

Paul went through over a year of getting sicker and sicker, slowly moving up the waiting list for a liver donor, with his love by his side (my mother Connie). Together they chose to do whatever was possible and take each day for what it's worth and not let time pass them by as they take on this overwhelming challenge. Paul told me, "We've been married for 10 years but we waited over 30 years to be with one another, so we have waited too long to be together for it to end now. And at the age of 50, this is inspiration enough to take on the fight." Paul chose to still live each day like it's his last by loving each morning sunrise and to keep pushing on.

The story of inspiration doesn't end here, Paul was lucky to be married to such a strong- willed and loving woman, my mother. A person has only so much motivation when you feel like you're losing the battle, especially when you're battling for your life. There were times he said to her, "I just don't think I'm going to make it," and she would say, "Yes you are, we just need to go through the bad times to get to the good and failure simply wasn't an option." She simply would not let him give up when he ran low on motivation. As his health deteriorated, she said there were times where he just didn't want to eat anymore so she would say, "I just won't eat either," and he would realize his decisions affected both of them and it usually worked.

Through several of the months while waiting for a transplant, he refused to go on disability income and he continued to work almost full time refusing to let his health stop him. He would continue on no matter what, by the strength and determination between both of them, through the ups and downs of the health problem.

After about a year of waiting for a donor, the clock started to tick faster as he reached a dangerous point of being toward the front of the waiting list, but was also becoming close to being too sick to receive a transplant and survive the operation. So they chose to be put on a waiting list in another state. Shortly after being put on their list, he found himself at the top of this list. They finally got the call they were waiting for, but it was not the call they hoped for. A gravely ill young lady had jumped ahead of Paul and the liver intended for him was transplanted into this deserving young lady. So Paul's Hepatologist started an all-night search for another organ that may save his life. One was found in Ohio, and Paul and my mother were flown on a mercy flight to the world renowned Cleveland Clinic for the operation. The liver transplant operation was a success and they removed the destroyed gallbladder too. However, 6 hours after the operation in ISU as they started to celebrate the victory against death, they discovered he had internal bleeding and he was soon bleeding faster than they could put blood back in him. It was coming out of his mouth, nose, and eyes, it was a nightmare. The doctors were stunned at the rate of blood loss and were almost at a loss on what to do other than open him back up. If there was a time to emotionally break down this was it, but not my mother Connie. As she stood in the back of the room crowded with doctors and nurses in a frenzy with several alarms going off, she calls out with a confident voice, "We just need to fix this." One of the head doctors said, "You heard her, we just need to fix this." They rushed him back into surgery and discovered a small tear in the back of the liver and they were able to mend it and save him, cheating death for a second time.

It would take more than a month of slow recovery before they could fly back to their home in Colorado, but on the last doctor visit for his free and clear check to go home, the cheers for success would be quickly taken away again. He was rapidly losing his strength to walk and move around. They ran some immediate tests and found he had a blood clot in the leg and it was extremely serious with the condition he's in. Talk about your setbacks. Connie even over heard two of the doctors talking about him and one said to the other, "He's not going to survive the blood clot, it's a shame after surviving the transplant." Well it turned out they were lucky to discover it when they did, and if luck would have it, there was a filter that was implanted in the artery months ago and was never taken out from another complication that he had, and it now saved his life by preventing the clot to continue up to his heart, which would have been fatal.

Doctors were able to clear the blood clot and save him once again, and Paul and Connie were finally able to go home once his strength returned enough.

The challenges Paul and Connie had to overcome in this ordeal were amazingly difficult, but how they worked through their struggles and never gave up had lasting effects, not only on them, but also everyone around them, including me. The doctors that worked on his case also invited Paul to talk in front of a panel of doctors about his story and how he survived.

Now, 10 years later, he is doing great, working full time in a rewarding career with the government, and is involved with others going through the life threatening challenge of needing a transplant. He also speaks on the topic to raise hope and show it is possible to not only survive it, but continue to live your life the way it was.

I asked him recently with everything he went through, how did it change him and he said, "It was an inspirational awakening." He continued to say it's difficult to put into words, but in the recovery room right after the surgery, "I all of a sudden felt more alive than I've ever been. I felt closer to my inner self, or spiritual self, than I've ever been. I sensed an outer force that I was connected to and that it had an influence over what happens; past, present, and future."

He said, "I would not be who I am today if it was not for what I went through. Overcoming such a challenge and having a sense of getting a second chance in life has had everlasting effects, and being able to overcome something that seemed impossible at the time, now changes my view of all my other challenges I've had and all that are yet to come."

My greatest take-away from Paul's story is our challenges make us who we are. Our challenges also have the ability to expand our vision and insight of everything, or if we allow it, they can chip away at our soul and damage who we are and who we inspire to become. But it's up to us to choose how we handle a problem, how we overcome it, and what we learn from it.

Overcoming Change

When I was in college, I had a friend that was a victim of a life-changing drunk driving accident. But it was not the story of the accident that has stuck with me all these years, it was how he faced life after the accident that made such a powerful impression on me and others. It shows us that we all have it within us to find happiness in our lives no matter what life may throw at us, even if it means a life-changing event.

I became friends with him in college when he was already 23 years old, but his accident happened back when he was 19. One night there was a party, and at this party there was alcohol and he had plenty to drink, but he made plans to have a designated driver to drive him and another friend home. What he didn't know was that things didn't work out as planned and this night would change his life forever.

The night was an endless list of laughs and fun and when the time came to go home, he chose to crawl in the back seat of the car and fall asleep for the ride home, along with another friend that rode in the front passenger seat. The driver, however, was not sober like planned and as you can imagine, the worst happened. While asleep in the back seat, the driver slammed into another car, and with him completely unaware of what was happening from the back seat, his body was slammed around inside the vehicle. The other 2 in the car escaped the accident with minimal injuries, but my friend's life would never be the same again. At the age of 19 he was now a quadriplegic.

What an enormous challenge to have to take on at such a young age where we find ourselves at the crossroads of adulthood, searching for love and trying to decide who we want to be when we grow up. Now he was faced with far more difficult challenges and choices to make, many simple choices you and I would take for granted, like getting around physically, feeding ourselves, bathing, and even earning a living.

This is truly an enormous crossroad for anyone to have to face and one that can make or break even the strongest willed individual. Although he was filled with doubt, sadness, and frustration, asking himself how could this happen to me and at such a young age, but he did not give up. With the love and support of family and friends, he made a choice to carry on and make the most of his life versus giving up and becoming a physical and emotional burden on everyone.

Financially he would be okay for the special care he would need because they were able to sue the liquor store company for selling alcohol to minors, but he still faced an uphill battle of how to live a normal life with his disability living a life as a quadriplegic.

When I met him in college, he had already been facing this challenge for 4 years and I was amazed at how well he had adapted to his limitations, to push forward in life and do what he wanted to do and not just watch time pass by. Here is a guy limited to an electric wheelchair with very little muscle use in his body, but he has his own home and was living with his girlfriend, he can drive a specially designed van for his needs, and was going to college to pursue a future in business. He had a great personality and was very positive and upbeat. I became close friends with him during our college years, and found that being around him seemed to continually inspire me. I would be astonished as I would learn more about his disabilities and how he found ways to work around them to live and love life to the best of his ability.

It was still heartbreaking to hear that deep down he would give up everything he has to have his body back, or that he confessed that when he first came to terms with his disability he assumed that he would never marry or have a family.

Well, never say never, because his high school sweetheart stood beside him during the hard times, moved in with him when he got his own place, and then the unbelievable happened…they got married! Being a part of that wedding was probably the most emotional wedding I'll ever experience. He once again showed me and everyone else, including himself, that anything is possible. But you can't let life intimidate you into giving up, you simple have to find a way.

We are all faced with problems and choices that have to be made all day long every day, but not everything is a life-changing challenge. With every problem we face, we have the opportunity to make an internal choice on how we are going to handle it, even from how we greet the day to how we end it. Life does not need to be one big challenge. Instead, we need to see what we can learn from our problems, and start looking at the positive side because everything affects everything.

Choosing to have a positive attitude and positive state of mind, no matter what life brings your way, can change the very life you live and the opportunities that are brought into your life.

Chapter II
Creating the Best Surroundings

II. Creating the Best Surroundings

Our personal surroundings that make up our living space and work environment can have a powerful influence on our level of success and happiness. It has a direct effect on our motivation and drive, energy level, productivity, and overall emotional state of mind.

Music, as an example, has been around since before times untold, and it is known as a way of expression and emotional stimulation for the heart and soul. You'll notice when you play music with a fun happy beat, it triggers thoughts of good times and joy. When you play a love song, it puts you in a mental place where you think of that special someone that brings love to your heart. Music can have immediate effects on our frame of mind. Music can be used in many ways, like calming our nerves from a long and difficult day, or to generate excitement and fill us full of energy, ready to take on the world.

Like music, there are many things in our daily surroundings that also affect our emotional state of mind and energy level. We typically don't realize these, but they can have a significant impact on us.

Our two primary spaces we spend most of our time in are our home and work place. Typically our spare time, or down time, dictates how much interest and energy we spend keeping up these surroundings the way we would like to. But what we don't realize is the affects it causes by continually not giving the space the attention it needs to give us the most effective and positive workspace, or the relaxing and peaceful home environment that we want and need.

Our personal environment, whether it is our workspace or home, is an incredibly important key to living life in a positive and peaceful state of mind. It can affect us on many levels we don't typically notice; like our energy level, efficiency, stress, happiness, peace of mind, and overall enjoyment of the space we're in and life itself.

As an example of how our workspace can affect us, I had a friend Seth I used to work with that we all called "organizationally challenged." He was incredibly good at what he did as a profession, had a great personality, and was a great family man, but if you walked into his office, it looked like a bomb went off. If you asked him about his workspace, he would simply say it was an organized mess and this was his way of keeping on top of everything he was working on or needed to keep at the front of his mind at the time. From what I could see, he must have to keep a lot of things on the front of his mind with that much paperwork stacked all over.

I don't want to simply say a person has to be clean and organized to be on top of their work, but if you knew Seth, there was more to the situation then his snappy come back calling it an organized mess, when it really looked more like a tornado went through there. The truth was he traveled a lot for his work which left him little time to keep his personal office space the way he really wanted it. On many occasions he had to reach out to others to confirm information or request the information he needed again since he misplaced it, which caused great frustration and loss of valuable work time for Seth. Now we all have days like this, but the other red flag that Seth's workspace was causing more harm than good, was when he admitted to me on several occasions about not feeling in control of his time or on top of his work and always feeling like no matter how many hours he put in, he couldn't reach the bottom of the stack of work to be done.

During lunch one day, Seth started talking through some things that were really slowing him down on a daily basis, and how much time in the day he's losing dealing with it. He mentioned how he has no filing system to track his expenses for work travel, which becomes a nightmare at the end of the month to figure out. He admitted trying to track down specific emails, files, or past sales results with his current way of "organizing" is simply not working anymore. We talked about how much time he loses driving into the office when he's not traveling, and he should consider working out of his home, but he has never looked into doing it. He complained about how slow his computer is and how it needs to be looked at before it crashes and looses all his data. The one that really topped the list was his wife was having a hard time handling him working such long days even when he was not traveling. The list went on for about 45 minutes and then I finally asked him, "How much time could you save if you fixed everything we just talked about?" Seth sat silently for a good minute or two and then went from being heavily frustrated to smiling from ear to ear, realizing what it would mean to take the time to fix what needs fixing. It was time to take a day to really step back and take a look at these problems and his work environment, and see what he can do about it.

Seth and I had lunch again about 6 weeks later, and he was excited to tell me about all his changes he had made to his way of organizing his daily work and time. He said I can stop making fun of his office now because the piles of papers are gone and his office is no longer designated as a natural disaster. Seth said, "I feel on top of my game, I feel organized and on top of all my projects instead of trying to keep up. I feel more energized and motivated, and I have more time to get my miscellaneous work done. I'm now working from home on Fridays and getting more done, and most importantly, I don't have to work so many evenings to catch up on work." Seth said that change is not always the easiest choice, but a necessary one.

Seth taught me how much of a difference change in a workspace can make in a person. I watched him go from being frustrated with his management of space, work, and time, to seeing him feel on top of his work, happier than ever, filled with more energy and enthusiasm for his work, and more personal time for his family.

Our personal surroundings are not just limited to physical space, it also includes the people we bring into our lives. The people we interact with and choose to be our friends in life will influence us on many levels. The more we interact with a person, the more we find ourselves absorbing parts of them and their personality as we are ever-changing ourselves. Have you ever noticed after hearing a co-worker or friend say a particular phrase or word you've never used before yourself, and after awhile hearing it over and over, you find yourself using it in your own conversations? This is why you always want to keep in mind what type of people you interact with on a daily basis, and try to bring the type of people into your personal circle you want to be around, and make changes when necessary.

Have you ever noticed when a really positive person with a big smile enters the room how it can affect the entire atmosphere of the room, including yourself? How about when you run into someone that is very negative in life and all they talk about is what's wrong today and what they hate in life this week. You walk away from that conversation with negative emotions and feelings, as if you took a piece of them with you.

To grow as a person in the direction you want to go, you want to surround yourself with the type of people that inspire the emotions and interest you're looking for, allowing their happiness and success to rub off on you. By adjusting what you can in your personal surroundings, including the people you interact with, you can adjust the world you live in.

When we talk about our surroundings, one of the most well known terms is "Fung Shui."

Fung Shui is pronounced "fung schway" and means wind and water, the forces that shape our landscapes. The concept of Fung Shui is at least 5,000 years old and is the ancient Chinese art of space arrangement that uses the laws of nature to determine things, like what to put where so you can feel more relaxed, be more productive, and get along with others better.

Fung Shui is also known as a short reference to an ancient Chinese poem which describes the ideal conditions of a place where life can thrive in harmony. If you were a Fung Shui master from the past, your job was to find the most ideal locations for villages, farms, and communities that had the best conditions to prosper and thrive. The master would take into consideration things like the landscape and the locations and shapes of the hills, mountains, and valleys. He would look at the fertility of the soil, availability of drinking water, sun and wind within the location, vegetation, and presence of fish and wild life. These were all key examples of what to take into consideration for an ideal community to be successful and thrive.

Today is not much different. If you build a house, for example, you're going to take into consideration where to build it in relation to where you work, how close you may be to the main city, and if the area offers all the necessities you're looking for like stores, restaurants, etc. You may even consider what side of the house is going to take on the morning or evening sun. If you're relocating your business, you're going to take many things into consideration geographically, from ease of access to location, visibility, and population of the surrounding area. Both of these examples demonstrate trying to create the most "Fung Shui" location and environment for your needs.

Our personal living and workspace are just as vital to our happiness and productivity today as it was centuries ago, and we can look much closer than just the location or design for the ideal environment to live or work in. Have you ever noticed the color of a room can create a certain tone or ambiance? How about the arrangement of the furniture, and how it can create an inviting atmosphere or create a cold and uncomfortable one?

Here are some things to consider when evaluating and arranging your workspace to empower you and create the type of surroundings that maximizes what you want out of the space, whether it's peace and relaxation or energy, efficiency, and inspiration.

Creating an Inspiring Workspace.

Organization: One of the strongest topics for setting the tone of a person's workspace is organization. If you're disorganized with how you conduct your business, whether it's filing things or working on tasks, the organization of the tools you use is going to affect you on many levels, including some you may not realize. A person usually knows if they are disorganized. They're going to have to work harder to keep up with the work flow and may actually put in more time because it takes more time to get the job done. What you may not realize is when you start or end the day disorganized, you're doing it with a negative tone because you're not on top of what's left to be done or what the priorities are for the next day. You simply find yourself working a conveyer belt of work just trying to keep pace with it. In this example, the work is controlling you versus you controlling the work. Now, by approaching your work with an organized method, no matter what type of work you're in, you can find yourself taking control of your work instead of your work controlling you. This kind of approach to work leads to a person that is much more positive and enthusiastic about coming in to work and leaving each day with a smile because of lower stress and anxiety over the work load, and a stronger sense of control and accomplishment.

What I'm getting at is if you leave your work not knowing what's left on the project or if everything was not done that needed to be completed, you subconsciously take it home with you and carry it until the next day. This can have a build-up effect until stress digs in, mistakes happen, and you reach a level of frustration with your work that causes you to look for change instead of embracing your work and improving your way of taking care of business, and enjoying the work you do. Being organized is probably the most noticeable change a person can make to improve their work day, but there are other things we can change to improve how we spend our 40 hours a week earning a living, which we will cover in the next few pages.

Position of Power: Everyone wants to feel in control of their work and their workspace. In an office setting, placing yourself in a position to face the entrance to your personal office or cubical can be key to feeling secure and in control of your workspace. One option if you don't have the ability to face the entrance to your workspace is to add a mirror to allow you to see behind you. Studies have shown that individuals that could not face the entrance to their workspace felt more insecure, uncomfortable, and less productive. The conflict here is fellow workers sitting near them or walking by could see and hear everything they do, which causes a defensive feeling of being concerned about being watched because their back is facing the world. Think about it, when your back is turned to the world, you can't see someone entering your space, including your boss, which means you could be caught off guard when they pay you a visit. Ultimately, the lack of feeling in control of a person's workspace affects their concentration, stress levels, and overall productivity. I understand not everyone works in an office setting, but take a step back for a moment and look at your workspace. See what changes you can make to allow you to feel more in control of your space, by the direction you face and the zone you consider your work area.

Lighting: Studies have shown that good lighting can help lower eye strain, increase energy, and even brighten moods. Natural sunlight is always a healthy choice to light up a work area, but it's not always bright and sunny out so we have to rely on artificial lighting to illuminate our workspace. Florescent lighting is not the best lighting to use, but it is typical found in an office space layout because of low energy cost. What you can do to improve the lighting is supplement the fixed lighting in your area by adding a desk light or lamp. Using only overhead lighting can be uncomfortable for the eyes and the desk light or lamp will help with this.

Bring the Outside In: To add comfort and have a lower stress work environment, here are 3 things to consider adding to your workspace to help bring the outside elements in, and create a more peaceful and comfortable work area.

1.) Plants- A study done by Washington State University shows plants help reduce stress. They project energy and life, they act as an air filter from nature absorbing air pollutants in the office, and have even shown to increase productivity and improve attentiveness.

2.) Outdoor View- Plenty of offices or cubicles don't have a window, but don't let that stop you from enjoying the beauty of the outdoors during work. A nice scenic or landscape print to hang in your workspace can not only help make up for the lack of a window view of the outdoors, but will help create a soothing and stress relieving visual escape like a window does. An additional advantage to art work is you can pick any kind of view you prefer, from a mountain view to an ocean view, the sky's the limit. When you pick a landscape picture to hang in your work area, make sure you pick one that generates peace when you look at it. You're looking for a stress reliever or a picture that inspires you and creates energy within you, you're looking to add some motivation to the space.

3.) Water- Incorporating water into your workspace is also a proven stress reliever. Some different ways you can add water to your work area is by using a desktop water fountain, artwork that includes an ocean view, waterfall, or river scene. Another option is to have water in one of your personal pictures on your desk, like a vacation picture with the ocean in the background or your children playing in the water. The calendar you hang up in your space also could be used as an option to add the element of water to the area.

Comfort and Personal Touch: We all want a workspace that is comfortable to work in, but also expresses who we are and what we're about. Adding your personal touch can actually make you feel more comfortable and productive. Here are 4 things to consider having in your space to help maximize your comfort level and add a personal touch.

1.) Personal Pictures- Having a couple of personal pictures of your family, friends, or even your pets, can be a perfect touch for your workspace. Nothing creates a stronger emotional boost or conversation starter than a favorite personal picture that reminds you of friends, family, or good times. There are some things to consider when choosing the right pictures to display for everyone to see. You want to keep in mind that this is a work environment. You don't want to portray the wrong image, for instance, bringing in a picture of you drinking and partying. What you do want to do is choose pictures that spark a smile every time you look at them. Some ideal choices are going to be pictures that include family or friends from a fun event, a favorite vacation, your children playing a sport, or a picture with your pets in it. Studies have shown how pets are an amazing positive emotional thing to have in our lives, and having a picture in our workspace to remind us of them and the unconditional love they offer us, can be a very positive and uplifting image to have on your desk. Also keep in mind when choosing your pictures, you can be even more effective to choose a picture that has nature or water in it to emphasize peace and relaxation. Or use an action shot like playing a sport to remind you of good times and encourage energy and motivation. The idea is to not simply hang portrait pictures of the kids or friends like mug shots of who's in your life, but to choose pictures that remind you of good times and that have an emotional affect on you. As an example, I have a picture of my 3 kids from our trip to Maui hanging up, and when I look at it, I think about the kids but also all the fun we had on the trip, and it acts as an emotional escape for me even if it's just for a minute when I look at it. I have another picture of my boat on the lake with my family on it. When I look at this picture, I see the countless hours of fun I've spent hanging out on the lake on the boat as a family, and it instantly brings a smile to my face because it's one of my favorite hobbies. The third picture I have on my desk is of my wife hugging my 2 Siberian Huskies in the backyard, and this picture generates great peace and love in my heart when I look at it. I think about all that unconditional love my wife and my dogs provide me, with a great big smile of joy on my face. Keep these examples in mind when you choose the next picture you want to hang in your workspace.

2.) Computer Desktop/Background Image- Like our personal pictures, the computer background we pick can have a direct effect on our energy or mood, so you want to choose carefully. With the desktop image, the sky is the limit for what you can put on there, from a neutral color background, to digital designs, landscape pictures, and of course, personal pictures. To choose the right image, I always suggest picking a picture that portrays the energy that you want to increase in your work environment, or one to counteract, depending on your needs. As an example, if you're finding more stress lately in your work, I would recommend using a stress relieving picture like a beautiful scenic shot that you love or maybe a favorite personal picture of a vacation shot with your family. As an example, I use pictures of Caribbean beaches for a calming picture. If you're finding yourself lacking in motivation lately, you may want to display a picture that fires you up like an action shot. An example would be using a picture that creates excitement within you, maybe it's a sport, or a favorite hobby, or something you're working toward. Another suggestion is to use a picture of your child playing a sport or maybe a nature shot showing your favorite animal that portrays strength, focus, and aggressiveness to boost energy. Because of my love for wolves, my personal favorite has always been to use an action shot of wolves to fire me up when I need a boost of motivation for a day or two, then I change the computer background back to an ocean scene for a feeling of peace. You don't have to keep the same image up every day, in fact, I recommend changing it depending on what your needs are to stimulate the emotion you're looking for today.

3.) Sound- An Australian scientific study found that high levels of noise and condensed work areas cause the "rats in a cage effect," which leads to less concentration and lower productivity. A noisy and condensed work area also means constant battling of distractions which leads to negative psychological and emotional reactions, including high blood pressure and increased stress levels. The lack of privacy with everyone hearing your phone conversations also creates a feeling of insecurity for the average person.

You may not be able to remodel your work area, but there are a couple of things you can do to counteract the noisy distractions or uncomfortable silence in the work area. Whether you're in a noisy or quiet work area, studies have proven music to be a positive emotional stimulation to motivate, lower stress, and increase productivity. Having a quiet personal radio playing in your workspace (at a volume for only you to hear) can help keep your attention in your personal workspace and give less attention to the other distractions outside your personal work zone, and keep a smile on your face throughout the day.

Another option is white noise, which is a constant sound or frequency to counteract another. You can use a small desk fan or water fountain to provide a good way to cancel out some of the miscellaneous sound distractions around you. If you work in a workspace that's too quiet for you, you can use a fan or fountain to help break the uncomfortable silence of an overly quiet workspace and create a sound buffer to add comfort for making those calls you need to make.

4.) Words of Motivation- This is one of my favorites! Words of inspiration can have a powerful effect on our emotional state of mind and energy level to motivate us in the work place, but only if we read them enough to become a part of us. Have you ever walked into an office or waiting area and noticed a motivational picture hanging up like a mountain climber with an inspiring phrase or word like "courage," "dedication," or "determination." Did you pause for a moment as you looked deeper into the meaning of the picture and phrase? You can add your own inspiring words into your workspace and you don't have to have a full size poster to do it. You can simply add an inspiring phrase or famous quote like "the only limitations in life are your imagination," or "be a voice of inspiration for change," or how about "fail until you succeed." The idea is to add a phrase or quote that motivates and resonates within you, to create the inspiration you want in your life like high energy, a never give up attitude, or for creativity.

You can get famous motivational phrases off of the internet or use one of my inspirational quotes listed later in this book. The idea is to hang it up where you see it every day to remind you of what's important to you to be successful and happy in your work. You could also take it a step further and frame it in a small picture frame to set on your desk or hang on the wall for others to see and share your inspiration. I've seen firsthand employees getting more respect and notice from fellow workers and management by displaying words of motivation or inspiration. It shows you have the interest to grow as a person, and the drive to do more and want more in life for yourself and others. I have one of my favorite quotes hanging on the wall over my desk at home that's 3 feet long and says, **"Life isn't about finding yourself, it's about CREATING yourself."**

Another way to boost motivation or help you engage with the right start and direction for the day, is to have an affirmation email or text that you send to yourself to read at the beginning of each day. We'll dive deeper into affirmations later in the book, but what I'm suggesting here is to have a short positive message you say to yourself that is written in present tense that defines the state of mind and focus you want to have for the day. Here are a couple of examples;

"My unique and creative talents and abilities flow through me."

"I will have a great day today. I am successful and appreciated, and I love what I do."

"I serve others to the best of my ability in all I say and do."

We can all agree that how we start the day can have a rippling effect on our focus and effort level for the entire day, so taking only a minute in the morning to help set the tone before you engage in your work (no matter what you do) can help you have the day you want to have by taking charge of your emotional state of mind. You're not allowing the morning challenges you face to dictate if you're going to have a good or bad day. Remember there is power in words.

Creating a Peaceful and Inspiring Home Environment.

Our home is a vital contribution to our lives. The place we call our home is not just a place of rest, it's our sanctuary from the world. It's a place to feel safe. It's where we can have peace to recharge our emotional batteries. Home is where we laugh, cry, and celebrate the most in our lives. It's a place where we can openly express ourselves and enjoy life with family and friends. It's where we can spend time celebrating life by doing the things we want to do in search of fulfillment out of our lives. It's where our life stories begin.

The reality is we live in an amazingly faced-paced society moving at a rate that makes it difficult to keep up with all the change. Time becomes one of our most precious commodities, so our time spent in our home can be very important to us and our overall health. The challenge is we often don't have the time, resources, or money to make the home just the way we would like it. But you don't have to remodel your home to have a sanctuary that offers the peace and comfort you want. There are simple things you can do to make your home a sanctuary of peace, love and inspiration.

The first step to a peaceful and inspiring home, is to make it a well maintained and clean home, which is a naturally more inviting and comfortable space to be in. Not just to you and your family, but also to your guests. It's hard to feel welcome in a home when you walk in and see clutter and disorganization. It creates unease for you and others as if they are disturbing you at a bad time because of the negative vibe it creates. Of course, having a peaceful and positive home environment is much more than just being clean and organized. There are several other things to keep in mind to create the best home environment for you and your family. Here are 3 helpful tips to evaluate a space and transform the energy of the room to the kind of environment you want to experience in the home.

1.) When you walk into the room, look at the colors of the room, from the walls to the furniture. Look at the layout of the furniture and the flow of space in the room. Then look at the items in the room, what it adds or takes away from the vibe you're trying to create in the room. Lastly, decide what kind of feeling or mood the room projects.

2.) Determine the use of the room, what you spend most of your time doing in the space, and the type of environment or energy you want to create in the space. Is it relaxation and comfort for a living room, or motivation and creativity for a den or home office?

3.) Determine what you can change within the room to transform the environment to what you really want out of the space. You'll find you don't always have to remodel a room to transform the feeling you get from it. Sometimes just changing the arrangement of the furniture, or adding a little color to emphasize the mood you're looking for, or perhaps painting the room, can completely transform an uninviting space to an inviting retreat within your home.

Our homes are made up of several rooms, but the 2 key rooms I want to emphasize are the living room space and the bedroom space. These have the greatest impact on the overall energy of the home. Later we will discuss how a deck or patio can be used as a great outdoor sanctuary for you.

Key Things for Creating a Peaceful and Inspiring Home Environment.

The Living Room: When you look at a room in the home, whether it's the family living room or a bedroom for a child, you first need to determine the vibe or energy and purpose of the room. The living room is traditionally the center point of the home, the greeting place, and where a lot of your time is spent. There are some key elements that you want to focus on to have a living room that offers the feeling of positive energy, love, peace, and sanctuary.

1.) Inviting furniture layout- offering a relaxing tone and proper placement to create a comfortable layout. The layout should allow you to see one another when you're sitting in the furniture verses different directions. The entrances to the living room area must feel wide and inviting, as if you placed the furniture in a way to help direct traffic flow in the home. You don't want the space to feel too cut off or cramped, which means being selective on how much furniture you have in the space to make it feel open and inviting, but at the same time having enough places for everyone in the family to sit. Fireplaces are a great addition to living rooms because fire is a proven visual to create a comfortable and warm feeling within us, creating a peaceful energy in the room when used.

2.) Colors- can play a big role in the vibe or feeling you want to create in a room by the colors used on the walls and within the furniture, and may be one of the easiest ways to alter the feeling you want to create in the room. After you have chosen the feeling you want to create, you will want to investigate what colors would help generate the emotion you want to create in that space. Subtle colors vs. bold and bright colors can also help avoid allowing the color choice to dominate the feeling you want in a room. The color blue represents water and can have a calming effect and bring the feeling of tranquility and peace. The color yellow projects bright, sunny, happy, and nourishing effects. Red is the color of passion and romance, and also courage, because it's the color of fire creating energy and joy. Green is the color of nature, and helps with creating the feeling of nature in the room, along with a feeling of growth, vibrancy, and nourishment for health. White represents the color of innocence, freshness, and new beginning like an empty paint canvas. Orange is known as a more subtle option over red and offers a more social energy with it, along with the feeling of openness and optimistic feelings. Brown, the color of wood, and creates the feeling of strength, stability and warmth. Pink represents a feeling of gentleness, loving, and a soothing feeling. Black, the color of night, is known to offer the feeling of unknown, infinite, and absorbing, creating the feeling of depth and strength. Grey represents the element of metal, and as a wall color offers a feeling of clear, detached, and neutral feelings.

3.) Good lighting-with natural light during the day and additional lamp lighting beyond the overhead lighting in the evening, this can brighten the area and the mood of the room, or set the tone for a soothing comfortable feeling with the right lamp placement for a cozy evening. Evaluate your space during the day with natural light and again at night. Determine if you're really letting enough natural light in or if you should change out those window blinds or curtains. In the evening when you have to rely on artificial lighting, take a step back from your space and see if it really offers enough light for the space. Ideally is to have two levels of lighting for a space like a living room. The first is to have enough bright light to see and do whatever you would like in the room, as if the sun was still up. The second is what I like to call the movie lighting. Have a lamp or 2 in the space that you can use for a dim and subtle lighting, like for the times you just want to create that warm evening inviting space that says go sit on the couch and read a book, or relax and snuggle up in front of the fireplace with your loved ones.

4.) Bringing the outside in- typically you have natural light and a view of the outside that helps bring the outside environment into the living room space. But what if you live in an apartment or would rather keep the shades on the windows down for privacy? You can help bring the element of nature and the outdoors into your space by adding plants, flowers, and the element of water utilizing an indoor water fountain. Another option, similar to the workspace, is to bring in pictures of nature and landscapes to draw in the outdoors into the space. All of these ideas can help create a more comfortable and inviting room to spend time in.

5.) Personal touch- is my favorite element to any room because this is how we truly personalize the space by adding pictures of the family, scenic paintings, or artworks that create the feeling and emotion you want to portray in the space, and of course, personal memorabilia or souvenirs that remind us of the good times we've had in life. All of these things help as reminders of what we're passionate about, and by adding visuals in the room, it is helping us keep these passions and feelings in the room, on the front of our minds, and in our hearts.

The Bedroom: Many of the things we talked about with the living room space can be applied to any room, but there are some differences with a bedroom space. This room plays a key role in your level of energy for each and every day, because this is the space where you start and end each day. It's where you reenergize and sort out your subconscious thoughts throughout the night through dreams. In fact, studies have shown lack of good sleep is one of the leading causes of stress in our lives. Lack of sleep affects our level of focus and concentration, stress, and overall energy level. Furniture layout can be important, you don't want to design a bedroom to look like an inviting hang out, if the real intention is to create a private sanctuary you can call your own space for finding peace and quiet to relax and sleep in. We spend a third of our lives sleeping in a world of dreams, and we awake every morning to take on a new day. Believe it or not, our surrounds in the bedroom will have an impact on our level of peace while we sleep. It's safe to say a soldier trying to sleep on the battlefield is not going to sleep as peacefully as they would in the safety of his or her own bed back at home, right? The bedroom is a place to increase and amplify our focus on aspects of our life like relaxation, love, and rejuvenation of the physical body and the mind. When you look at your bedroom, consider the vibe it gives off when you enter the room and when you lay in bed. What is the last thing you see when you close your eyes? Is it a picture of the family on the wall, a painting that creates a warm peaceful feeling in your heart, or is it a pile of clothes on the chair or a pile of things to deal with in the corner? All of these things have an effect on our mind and the level of peace we take with us when we fall asleep. Every little thing that affects your thoughts can affect your sleep. As an example, if you have an alarm clock that isn't working right and you can't rely on it, you're going to worry all night long if it's going to wake you up in time for work. Keep in mind the layout of the furniture in the room, or the color of the walls and bedspread you choose, can all play a role in the energy and peace you can create in the space. Personal pictures, soft natural colors, and soft lighting like added lamps for toned down lighting for a quiet book read before bed, are all key things to look at adjusting, but don't overlook the bed itself. A comfortable bed and pillow have the greatest impact on your sleep because it affects your physical comfort level. Take an hour or two from one of your weekends and use the time to create the peaceful sleeping sanctuary you deserve, and feel the difference.

Patios and Decks: Not all of us have time in our schedule to enjoy the outdoors as much as we would like. That's why I believe our patios and decks at our home play a key role in allowing us small amounts of time to enjoy the fresh air and sunshine. Here are a couple of tips to make a positive and enjoyable outdoor oasis. Make sure your outdoor space does not become cluttered, or filled up with too much outdoor furniture to help create an inviting, clean, and peaceful outdoor experience. Adding flowers and plants can also add a great touch of nature to your space, especially if your patio or deck does not have a good view of nature, like an apartment balcony. So bringing nature to you is the next best thing. We all can't afford a view of the ocean, but adding a small water fountain is a great way of adding the peaceful element of water into the space, and the sound it offers can help relax us. Choose outdoor furniture that is comfortable enough for you to want to be outside as long as your heart desires. If the direction of the sun limits your available time in the space, look for ways to shade the area, allowing for a cooler and more comfortable setting to relax and enjoy.

There are plenty of spaces that you will want to apply the same suggested points to that we have touched on, including the kitchen, bathrooms, front entrance, and even the garage. If you utilize these suggestions to any room or area of the home, I'm confident you will create the ideal sanctuary for you and your family with an abundance of peace, harmony, positive energy, and love in your home that will call to you every time you walk in the front door.

Chapter III
The Power of Positive Thinking

III. The Power of Positive Thinking

"Life is not about what you see, it's about how you see it." This is one of my favorite reflections on life, and is a key to a person's happiness. This quote hits the true core of what has the greatest effect on the world we choose to live in, because how we choose to see the world defines the way we live. Life is all about choices and you have the power within you to be successful and happy, because happiness is a conscious choice we make with everything we see and do in our lives. It's not something we can buy or own, it's a frame of mind. This is the <u>1st key to empowering yourself with positive thinking, which is having a positive state of mind and perspective at all times.</u>

Life is challenging no matter who you are and where you live, but that doesn't mean a person can't live a life that's abundant with happiness, fulfillment, and success. I believe the true challenge is to rise above the obstacles in life and embrace our personal challenges and problems. Learn to view these things as lessons in our lives, to teach and inspire us to become better with each step we take in life. This all starts with the power of positive thinking and seeing the light in even the darkest of moments. We should not allow our problems in life to chip away at who we are. Instead, we need to allow them to teach us life so we can emerge as a stronger, wiser, and greater person then before. Of course, looking at one's path and walking it are two different things. This is where positive thinking plays a crucial role. Facing life with the right frame of mind can make all the difference in the world. As I like to say, **"You can't frown and smile at the same time, so why not choose to smile."**

The reality is how we view our life defines the kind of life we live. So why not look for the good in everyone and everything, and see the potential in every moment. When you lose your job because of company cut backs, you can choose to hate your former employer for making choices like this that can affect your financial well-being, or you can choose to see it as an opportunity for life to show you another path to take. This allows you to look at where you are currently in life, where you want to be, and what new path will lead you there that could be better than what you were doing before.

What about when a person who is injured in a horrible car accident discovers they will never walk again? Life is not punishing them, it's presenting them with a challenge and lesson in life. A person can choose to slip into the darkness of depression, filled with anger and hate toward life because life will never be the same, or they can choose to rise again and look for meaning in their life behind such a change. It makes you look at who you are to discover the new life that has been handed to you and learn to discover new ways to enjoy life. They said it best in the last Rocky movie when Rocky said, "Life isn't about how hard you're hit, it's about how hard you can get hit and keep moving forward, how much you can take and keep moving …that's how winning is done." Our challenges in life don't define who we are, these are the opportunities to learn and grow from. How we choose to rise from our challenges when life knocks us down, that defines who we are.

Here is an exercise to try. Take a look at the following picture for just a few seconds and then continue reading.

Now that you took a glance at the picture, what did you focus on first? Did you immediately gravitate your attention to the storm approaching, or did you first focus on the people enjoying themselves in the warm Caribbean clear blue waters and rolling grass hills in the distance? What was your first reaction to the picture? Were you thinking about the storm coming and the dangers, or were you first thinking about the fun and joy the people were experiencing in such a beautiful paradise location?

The exercise was to see if you looked at the good or the bad in the picture. The goal with positive thinking is to train yourself to instinctively always look for the good in every situation and not what's wrong with it. It's up to you to decide if the glass is half full or half empty.

The key is to learn to see the good side and opportunity to every situation in life. You need to discipline and train the mind to continually look at the positive side of every moment. When you look at the positive of even the worst of circumstances, your mind will be more open to see the opportunity and good that you can draw from the moment, because your mind will be unblocked by the impact of negative emotions like anger, hate, regret, sorrow, depression, fear, or sadness. When you master focusing on the positive side of things, it will allow you to live a much happier and fulfilling life. You won't be wasting countless hours of negative thoughts that cause the negative emotions that will also have an effect on you with stress and anxiety. Nothing can compare to the amazing joy you feel by living a life fueled by positive thought. You feel more in control of your life. You are happier, more grateful, and more at peace with yourself, feeling ready to take on the world with a feeling of certainty and security. Positive thinking can empower you and help eliminate social and sociological barriers by freeing the mind from negative conceptions of yourself, others, and life itself.

A person is challenged from every angle, from physically to emotionally to physiologically. Now we may not be able to control the outcome of the moment, but we can certainly choose how we choose to face it, deal with it, and except it, and that has an ever-lasting effect on who we are and who we become. If you're driving to work and someone cuts you off and creates a moment of danger for you, do you hold onto that anger and keep replaying the moment in your head dwelling on it? When you get to work, do you tell the first couple of co-workers you see about the incident on the road 20 minutes ago and how angry you are about it? Or do you choose to let go of the moment and not dwell on it and not fuel your emotions of anger toward what happened. You choose whether or not to allow something to affect you. Remember, **"A person's true character is defined within the challenges they face, and how they face it."**

Positive thinking is not just happy thoughts like Peter Pan uses to fly, it's much more. It's having the right state of mind or perspective on each moment so you can not only see the silver lining in any situation, but to empower yourself to be happy no matter what happens. The 2nd key to empowering yourself with positive thinking is to become **"emotionally aware"** of your thoughts and emotions. We do this by conditioning ourselves to be aware of the emotions we feel and the emotions we choose to hang onto for any moment or problem we face. The goal is to be happy and believe in life and in yourself no matter what life is challenging you with. Allow yourself to see the bigger picture in difficult moments and see the opportunity it brings to you so you can learn and evolve as a person. As they say, **"There's no perfect life, there's just life."** So it's up to you to choose to embrace it and enjoy it, but you can only do that if you embrace the right emotions behind it. When you're playing a sport and lose the game, it's up to you alone to choose to be upset and angry at yourself for losing, or to concentrate on the positive which is having fun playing the sport and discovering why you lost so you can potentially win next time.

So how do we become **"emotionally aware"** of ourselves? You first have to become more aware of your emotional state of mind when facing a problem or challenge in life, no matter how big or small it is. Become disciplined in taking a moment of pause, take a deep breath, and feel out your true emotions for the moment or situation you face, and find the right emotion. You're looking for the positive emotion to embrace the moment with. No matter how dark the situation is, you can focus on the good. With this approach, you become thankful for the challenges in life because your problems (big or small) now become beautiful gifts and lessons of life. I believe one of the true meanings of life itself is, **"We live to learn so we may learn to live."** The key here is it's difficult to learn from life if you refuse to embrace life with an open mind, and to do so, you need to rid yourself of the negative emotions. Have you ever noticed how it's difficult to finish something you're doing if you're really angry about something else? You can't concentrate, and you find yourself continually thinking about how angry you are.

Here is another example of allowing negative emotions to take control of you, and not being emotional aware of yourself and your reactions to the moment. Do you ever notice when you're angry it's easy to lash out with harsh words to a loved one, but afterwards you regret it? If you had to do it over again, you probably would've liked to have been more in control of yourself and would have responded differently to the situation.

Whether you mean to or not, everything you give attention to, talk about, or get emotionally involved in, you invite internally into yourself mentally and emotionally. It will affect you not only emotionally, but also physically, and spiritually. As an example, we watch the news to hear what's happening in our community. But the news is filled with top stories of all the bad things that are transpiring, and they cover very few stories of the great accomplishments that are going on in the world. We have a choice of what we spend our energy focusing on and absorbing. We need to condition ourselves to not act like a news channel focusing all our time on what's gone wrong today, and spend our time focusing on what's going right. You will see a difference in your emotional state of mind and even in your level of motivation and energy for the day. You'll have less stress and anxiety, and overall greater level of peace of mind, and *that's* the real goal here.

How we think about things, and even more importantly ourselves, are very important. This leads us to the <u>3rd key to empowering yourself with positive thinking, which is believe, respect, and love for yourself and who you are.</u> How we view ourselves and by believing in ourselves is critical. By telling yourself, "I can't do this," or "I'm stupid," or "I'm never going to get this, it's impossible," you're basically telling yourself that this is your reality, this is fact, so it becomes true and you train-wreck your own success. We are our own worst critic, and we need to realize saying things like this to ourselves will make it a reality. When in fact, it's the exact opposite from what we really want to have happen. This is the instinctive behavior of focusing on what's wrong with a situation, and this is what we need to change. What we need to do is spend most of our energy and thoughts focusing on what we want the outcome to be and not what's going wrong. We need to believe in ourselves, that we *can* accomplishment things. If you believe in yourself with all your heart, then you're making a conscious choice to not allow outside influences to affect accomplishing what you want. Do you think Michael Phelps, who won 16 Olympic medals in swimming during the 2004 and 2008 Olympic Games, won by telling himself that this is impossible and I can't possibly do this? Or do you think he believed in himself and visualized himself winning the gold, and he pushed past any obstacles that stood in his way to become the world's best Olympic swimmer.

The real challenge in today's society is it's moving so fast that we really don't take the time to think about ourselves and what we really want out of life. If we really want to live a fulfilling and happy life, we need to first adjust our approach to life. Try approaching life with a positive mind and attitude, and take the time to reflect to determine what we really want. Take control of your perspective on life, then you can conquer your fears and reach new heights in all aspects of your life. This is the <u>4th key to empowering yourself with positive thinking, which is take time to reflect and believe in yourself</u>.

Before a music diva walks on stage, or before a professional boxer takes to the ring, they empower themselves with words of inspiration to believe in themselves. They visualize the standing ovation; they visualize winning the boxing match. They tell themselves, "I can do this, this is who I am." You have to take the time to program your mind into believing you can do it. If you have a goal in life you're trying to achieve, take a minute each morning and remind yourself that you can do it and to believe in yourself. This is where affirmations can be very powerful, which we will get to later in another chapter. Just remember, **"When your thoughts and intent are clear, your thoughts will become reality."**

Chapter IV
The 12 Key Elements for Success and Happiness

IV. The 12 Key Elements for Success and Happiness

The key components for living a positive, fulfilling, and successful life.

To live the dream, that ideal life we envision in our mind, filled with happiness, peace, love, success, and overall fulfillment, we need to understand what the key components are to make the dream a reality. You can have everything and still feel like you have nothing without understanding the key elements to a successful and happy life. You can't live without compassion in your heart, you can't enjoy life if you don't express joy through laughter, you can't have success if you don't believe in yourself and what you've accomplished in life, and you can't have peace without peace in your heart and mind. In the pages ahead, we will explore the 12 key elements necessary for living a positive and fulfilling life filled with success and happiness.

1. Thoughts are Things- Everything starts with a thought. What we believe, think, and envision in our mind is the beginning to our actions and reality we choose to live in.

One of the greatest keys to happiness is the state of mind in which you choose to live in. Everything starts with a thought; you don't walk across a room without thinking about it first, and having thoughts about where you're headed and why.

The key lies within how you think about things. There are always two ways to look at things, and a person has to decide if they're going to focus on the negative or the positive side of every moment, or to dwell on what's going wrong or what's going right.

If you think about it, it's difficult to be angry or cry if you're holding a smile, and the truth is the smile goes deeper than the grin on your face. When you smile, you're making a conscious decision to physically express the emotion of happiness, which naturally leads to positive thoughts and emotions. It's these emotions that can affect us physically and sociologically, so how we think about things is where the magic lies.

On any given day, a person could easily make a list of all the problems they faced that day, but would struggle to make a list of all the positive moments they had. So we need to ask ourselves…why is that? It's because we typically focus on our roadblocks that get in the way of our goals for the day, instead of spending our time focusing on the positive elements of each moment and what they mean to us.

It's a natural thinking process to think about the problems you need to face and how to overcome them. The real problem lies with a person focusing all their energy on what's wrong with every situation and all the "what if" scenarios, that they miss seeing the opportunities and the positive side to any moment. A good example is next time when you're sitting among co-workers or friends, ask them to share some of their worst experiences on the road traveling cross country, or maybe flying. I would venture to bet that everyone would have several stories to share and at least one in the group that could spend all day talking about problems they've had with their travels. Now, the second question to ask the group is to share some of the best experiences they've had traveling, and you'll find they will have a much more difficult time recalling just as many positive and fun stories to share as they did negative ones.

We need to move past spending so much mental energy on what's wrong or what could go wrong, and just live in the moment and focus on the positive side of any challenge we face. If you can do that, then even if you lose, you win, because you can see what you can get out of even a bad situation, and that's positive thinking.

The key is to remember that "thoughts are things" and what you focus on is what you're attracting into your life, also known as the law of attraction. When you focus on something you truly want in life and have made a firm decision in your mind, you will find yourself seeing and attracting the things that correlate with what you want or need to make your thoughts come true. Here's an example; think back to a time when you wanted to purchase a particular kind of car and you have been giving it some serious thought. I would be willing to bet you started noticing all the cars on the road that was the make and model you wanted, as if they all stood out from the rest of the traffic. It's because you were focusing on it subconsciously, not just consciously. You listed the car on what I like to call the "internal focus list." This is the list your subconscious is focusing on for you, because you've giving the thought enough focus to render it important in your mind. The catch is not to put things on your "internal focus list" you don't want, because the law of attraction also applies if you give something enough attention that happens to be the opposite of what you want.

Your mind, body, and spirit need to be in sync. Do you think you can hit a golf ball straight down the fairway if you're thinking nonstop about the trees to the side; or how can you lose weight, if all you can think about is food? What we focus on in our mind plays a crucial part in the outcome, so we need to train ourselves to focus on what we want, and not what we don't want. Simply put, be mindful of your thoughts. Here's an example; say a child is playing baseball and he steps up to the plate and takes his stance ready to swing the bat, but all he/she can think of is, "what if I miss," or "they throw too fast for me," or "I'm going to strike out." What do you think the odds are the child is going to hit the ball when they are telling themselves they can't do it? The body will listen to the brain, but you have to tell the brain what you want, not what you don't want. You need to tell yourself, "I can do this." Visualize the ball flying over second base and landing in the outfield. Bottom line is being mindful of what you focus your mind on and how you think about it.

Visualization also magnifies your thoughts on what you want, like I mentioned in the baseball analogy. Take the time to think through what you want out of a situation AND visualize yourself achieving it. Don't just think about the house you want to buy, or the 20 pounds you want to lose; give your mind a deeper thought of what you want to become your reality. Visualize yourself walking through the front door of the house you want to buy, or visualizing yourself after you've successfully lost the body weight and how great you look. You can make the goal more defined and real in your mind because you're telling yourself this is what I want for my reality, and this WILL be the outcome because in your mind you have already made it happen.

Remember "thoughts are things," so control what you focus on. If you want to live a positive and happy lifestyle, then you want to be emotionally aware of how many negative thoughts you allow in, and not lose sight of the positive side of things. Focus your mind on believing in yourself and life, be optimistic, and live with compassion in your heart and in your actions.

2. Responsibility- Acceptance and taking responsibility empowers you to take control of your life.

To live a life of happiness, a person needs to take responsibility for their actions. We need to learn to focus on the solution, and not the problem. We need to learn to let go of any thoughts of whom or what is to blame for the problem and just take action to resolve it.

Anyone can point the blame at another person or a set of circumstances for why things are not working out. But how much time and emotional energy do you want to waste dwelling on blame and what went wrong? Life is not perfect, and taking responsibility is allowing you to have the right frame of mind to take action and change the situation by choosing to move forward. We also have to recognize it's not about what went wrong, like lack of money, time, support, economy, resources, and the final straw that caused the collapse of failure in the situation. **It's about your resourcefulness and determination to succeed.** With the right frame of mind, anything is possible.

We all have challenges in our life, but you can't allow the challenges to win over you. Don't let the problem take control of you, you take control of the problem. History is filled with lessons that show us that the ones that are most determined to win their fight will indeed succeed. Take Mr. Superman, Christopher Reeve, for example. Here is a person with a fantastic movie career as the Man of Steel with super powers. Even the Man of Steel was faced with great challenges of life, as he was crippled and paralyzed for life by a horse riding accident during a horse jumping competition in 1995. Christopher was faced with a choice, live in a life of pain and sorrow blaming himself for allowing the accident to happen, or take hold of his life again (as difficult as it was) and fight on. He took responsibility and acceptance for his life and health to prove to the world he could live on, and would live a life worth living again filled with smiles and laughter. Christopher found a new way to shine for humanity by putting a face on spinal cord injuries, and motivated neuroscientists around the world to conquer one of the most complex diseases of the brain and central nervous system. He became a spokesman and inspirational icon for many others around the world fighting spinal cord injuries, and other serious physical challenges. He inspired people to fight on, live life, and never give up, no matter what physical challenges you face. Life is ever changing, and we need to continually rise to the challenge of change in our life and keep moving forward by owning the problem and living the solution.

You may not be able to control the fact that you lost a loved one to a car accident, or have to battle cancer, or you got laid off from your job, but you can control how you accept it and deal with it. Acceptance is an important step in allowing you to take responsibility for your life and actions, to empower you to take control of your life from within.

No matter how difficult of a problem you may be facing, just remember this, somewhere there is someone fighting an even greater fight, and they are choosing to stand tall. It's up to you alone to take the responsibility of your life into your own hands and find the strength within to live on and find the meaning of the challenges you face. **"Remember to live life as a lesson of love and NOT a battle to survive, otherwise you lose the meaning in the fight and in life itself."**

3. Compassion- All actions, thoughts, and words in one's life should be driven by compassion, pride, and joy.

What is life without compassion? It's the driving purpose of why we do things. We are not a species that survives on instinctive thought, like a colony of ants, but rather a species capable of amazing independent thought and reasoning, driven by our compassion and love for life and all that is in it. Think about it, do you hug a family member simply because it's custom, or do you hug them to express your love and compassion for them? Do you mow and trim your yard simply because it's Saturday, or do you groom your yard because you care what it looks like and want it to look beautiful? If you see an elderly person struggling with something, do you ignore them, or do you help them because you care and you don't want to see another person struggle in pain? Our lives are filled with tasks we may not want to do, like cleaning our home, helping our child with difficult homework, dealing with bills, miscellaneous problems, or maybe even our job or career itself. The key is to look for the meaning behind the action, then you can see the beauty in anything in life you do, and find the compassion and purpose within it. Compassion should be the driving force behind the type of job we choose to work, so we can enjoy what we do and all the little things within it. I believe compassion is also a crucial tipping point in helping a person shift from disliking, or only being satisfied with their job, to truly enjoying and loving what they do.

Several studies have shown people that love what they do for a job, and have a passion for their career, typically have the following key elements in their job.
- They are *challenged,* creating daily interest.
- The job offers *variety,* offering more than one task to enjoy doing.
- It has some level of *independence,* so you have a voice and a choice in what you do and how you do it.
- The company or job offers the *opportunity to continually learn something new,* maybe expanding your expertise in your job function, or in additional areas of the company so you can continual grow your knowledge.

- They have a *great boss and/or co-workers.* If you don't like the people you work with and work for, then the rest just will not add up to an enjoyable job.
- *Management that leads and inspires their workers* and not just manages business.
- Find *work that matters to you and/or finding the meaning behind the job function you can connect with.* For example, you may work in accounting at a life insurance company, so perhaps you find the compassion behind the work you do because you love accounting, and that you work for a company that sells life insurance, which helps people in the moment of financial need when a loved one passes.

Did you notice that money was not on the list? What was interesting was the individuals that love what they do are also the ones that are typically very positive people. What was also discovered through all this research was it's not about finding the perfect job. You don't have to be a surgeon saving lives to have the greatest job on earth. You can be a garbage man and love what you do. If you love being outside and on the road versus in an office with management looking over your shoulder, then this could be the perfect job for you. A person has the power to choose to have compassion for their work. It's all about internal choices and how we choose to see things.

Life is not easy and we all certainly have things in our life we don't want, or perhaps don't want to deal with. But if we have compassion in all our actions and words, and always care about what we're doing and the reason for doing it, then you will live a fulfilling life because we will no longer feel as if we're wasting our time with anything. You'll try your best at everything you do because you care, and you will see your life transform into the life you want and envision it to be.

4. **Laughter**- See the joy in every moment life brings you and express your happiness with laughter and smiles to live a life filled with joy.

Laughter has been described as one of the most contagious things. A smile can light up a room with positive emotions because it's the expression of joy and happiness. We have all heard the saying, "laughter is the best medicine." Laughter creates a positive and happy state of mind that in turn creates physical chemical changes within the body that leads to several impressive health benefits. Studies have proven that laughter truly is the best medicine because it can naturally lower stress, blood pressure, and much more. It's actually difficult to summarize all the benefits a good laugh can do for us, but here are some of the great benefits we need to recognize so we can quantify just how much it affects us.

Benefits of Laughter:
- **Positive frame of mind-** A good laugh redirects our thoughts away from negative emotions and can place a person in an instant positive state of mind.
- **Increases energy levels-** Laughter naturally reenergizes us and increases our energy levels because a hardy laugh will increase our heart rate and make us more alert.
- **Exercising with laughter-** Studies has proven that 100 good laughs will have the same effect on the body as 10 minutes on a rowing machine, or 15 minutes on a stationary bike. Laughing is the easiest way to burn calories.
- **It helps connect us with others-** It allows us to put down our defenses like fear, tension, anxiety, and even anger. Research also shows when we laugh with our friends or family it allows for a stronger personal connection and it helps strengthen our bond with the people around us.

- **Talking-** Laughter helps us engage more in conversations, retain more information, make better eye contact, and have a greater interest to talk more.
- **Combats stress-** A large portion of a person's stress level is related to how we think, and when a person is stressed, they have higher levels of stress hormones like Cortical. Laughter has been proven to lower levels of Cortical, which helps us cope with stressful situations.
- **Reduces blood pressure-** Research shows that laughter can reduce blood pressure and allow people to handle stressful situations better.
- **Emotional rebalance-** A good laugh allows a person to physically and emotionally release their feelings, allowing a person to feel more open and connected with the moment.
- **Strengthens the immune system-** Research and studies show laughter increases our antibody producing cells, increases efficiency of T-cells, and increases levels of Salivary Immunoglobin A used to fight off bacteria and viruses. Laughter allows for an overall stronger immune system so you're capable of fighting off illnesses better. Less stress and more laughter also means less physical effects on the body.
- **Natural pain reliever-** One of the most powerful chemical substances in the body is endorphins. This group of natural chemicals, that includes serotonin, is also a natural pain reliever within the body and laughter increases these levels.

Laughter is truly a powerful element to living a happy life with it affecting our mind, body, and spirit. So always look for the bright side to every moment, laugh often, laugh loud, and laugh proud.

5. Gratitude- Always be grateful. Gratitude leads to joy and peace of mind, allowing you to be free from the burdens of the wants and needs of life.

Gratitude allows you to accept things for what they are and be happy, unlocking joy in your heart no matter what the situation brings. It calms the mind by allowing you to except the situation and not give attention to the negative emotions like frustration, dissatisfaction, fear, anger, greed, or hate. You're choosing to accept the situation for what it is by being grateful for what it is and not what it could be. Gratitude helps keep us humble. Keep in mind, no matter what struggles you face or what problems you endure in life, there is always someone else fighting a greater fight, so you are not alone. There is always something to be grateful for.

- If you lose your job, be grateful for your family and health.
- If you get in a car accident and break your leg, be glad you're still alive.
- If you're fighting a disease, be thankful for having loved ones to support you.
- If you've lost everything, be grateful you still have your life and health.
- If you're battling weight gain, just remember there's someone struggling to live another day from lack of food and nutrition.
- If you're terminally ill, be thankful you have time left to share a few more moments with the people close to you and reflect on your wonderful life.

Gratitude is so important because it allows us to accept life's challenges in a positive light, and this can affect us on every level physically, physiologically, and spiritually.

Always remember gratitude allows acceptance, which leads to joy and peace of mind.

6. Optimism- Always be optimistic no matter what challenges you face. Optimism will allow you to see beyond a problem to find the benefits of any moment.

To live a positive and happy life, always be optimistic no matter what challenges you face, and good will come from it if you choose to see the benefits of every moment.

Every challenge you face in life can be considered a gift and opportunity to grow, or a problem and an obstacle to deal with, but the choice is yours. Studies show that optimistic people will look at situations differently than pessimistic individuals, and can lead to different ways of approaching and dealing with a situation, which can ultimately lead to a different outcome.

Pessimistic individuals tend to see things as more black and white and focus more on what could go wrong in a situation versus the goal, leading to more time spent contingency planning and worrying about the "what if" factor. They tend to notice problems as obstacles versus seeing the opportunities of a situation, and because of this thought process, they live with more concern and frustration in their daily life.

Some people would say they are not a pessimist, but a realist. But I would argue that an optimist is also a realist, but they choose to focus on what they want and not what could go wrong, and live with more belief in their heart, that one way or another, good will come from any situation.

Optimistic people tend to see problems as opportunities and not black and white situations that can or cannot be done. They believe there is always a way and there's always a solution to every problem. An optimistic person believes with every dead end there's a way out, and they don't focus on what could go wrong or worst case scenarios for outcomes, but rather focus on what can be done and believe anything is possible. This is the frame of mind you want to train your mind to take, and over time when you choose to look at enough situations with this point of view, you will naturally start looking at situations with optimism.

7. Believe- To truly be happy and successful in life, you need to have faith and believe! Believe in yourself, others, and life itself.

Belief and faith in life are your fuel for motivation. It gives you direction and wind in your sails, without it you would be lost at sea. Belief plays a big part in our lives even if we don't realize just how much we utilize it. Would you jump off a rock if you didn't believe you would be okay? Would you choose to apply for that job if you didn't believe you could do it first?

To succeed in life you first have to believe in yourself. Belief gives us the motivation to make the impossible, possible. After all, if we didn't think we could accomplish something then we wouldn't even try. Do you think the Wright brothers would have built the first powered flying contraption, better known as the airplane, if they didn't believe in themselves and the possibility that mankind could fly? Belief gives us hope and inspiration to push on no matter what the odds are and the outcome is uncertain, except for the belief in your heart and mind.

Belief in one another is also very important. It's our human nature to learn and evolve, and everyone we come in contact with teaches us about life, good and bad. We need to believe in each other if we are going to trust and learn from one another in this great adventure we call life, and it all starts with believing.

A wise man once said, "The only untrustworthy person is a person you're not willing to trust." Humanity is an amazingly beautiful and compassionate race of life, but we act and react too often in fear or anger for many reasons, like self preservation, personal greed, or emotional rebalancing from personal challenges we've faced. This causes us to react differently than we know to be the right reaction. We need to trust and believe to help each other succeed in our challenges. Realized or not, we are all connected in life, and if you can believe and support one another, the world will become a better place. My favorite expression in life is, "**Have faith**." Have faith in life and believe in yourself, and in other people, and you will see the world through heaven's eyes.

8. Self Improvement- Life is about self improvement, mentally, physically, and spiritually. To love yourself, you need to take care of yourself, challenge yourself, and keep growing.

We all want to improve ourselves in every aspect of the word. It's human nature to be in a continual search to learn and evolve as a person. The challenge is today's society is moving so fast that we don't truly devote enough time for self improvement. We spend so much time just trying to keep up with our family, careers, technology, having that next best thing that will simplify our life, or getting to that next place on time. We take on so much in our lives that most people I know are basically chasing their tails just trying to keep up with life. Think about it, the average person takes a vacation to escape their life and relax for a week just to catch their breath. But the truth is if you come back to your life after a great vacation and become even more frustrated with your life, then clearly some things are not in balance with the way you're living your life.

We work so hard on our lives with the best intentions. We're trying to move up the ladder in our job or career to have a better life and/or provide a better life for our families, but what we're usually overlooking is **ourselves!** Take the time to expand who you are and your interests. We all pretty much know what needs attention in our lives, or what we want to spend more time learning about or experiencing, but we typically put ourselves low on the priority list because we're so busy with everything else. Think about it, are you on the low end of your own priority list?

If your body is aging too fast, maybe that means you join a health club. If your weight is a concern and you haven't given it a real focus, maybe it's time to take a pause and address it. Simply saying you don't have time for yourself is crazy. If you want to expand your knowledge on a topic you would love to learn more about, maybe it's time to pick up a book, search the web, or take a class in your community or nearby college. If you're passionate about a cause, maybe it's time to get involved instead of saying "someday." Make today the "someday." Do what brings a smile to your face and expands who you are mentally, physically, and spiritually.

Here is my challenge for you: Take the time to expand who you are and your interests so you start spending time doing the things you want to do, and become the person you envision to be. Take at least 20 minutes right now and make 2 lists with the following directions on the next couple of pages.

List 1: Make a list of what needs attention in your life.
Maybe you're not at your ideal weight, or you would like to exercise more and become more fit. Maybe you have health concerns you've been avoiding. Perhaps you want to devote more time with your spouse or family. Whatever comes to mind that you believe needs attention in life, physically, spiritually, maybe financially, put it on the list.

List 2: List your interests you enjoy doing, and are compassionate about.
Maybe it's church, or devoting time to a charity of interest. How about a hobby or favorite past time like painting, gardening, or woodworking. How about spending time learning more about a topic you love, perhaps a period in history, technology. Whatever brings joy to your heart when you think of spending time doing it, put it on the list.

List 1: Make a list of what needs attention in your life.

1.
2.
3.
4.
5.
6.
7.
8.
9.
10.
11.
12.
13.
14.
15.
16.
17.
18.
19.
20.

List 2: List your interests you enjoy doing, and are compassionate about.

1.
2.
3.
4.
5.
6.
7.
8.
9.
10.
11.
12.
13.
14.
15.
16.
17.
18.
19.
20.

Now I challenge you to take action on one thing from each list today to work on over the next few weeks. You don't have to rebuild your life overnight. But I bet if you take on one challenge from each list that you want to improve, try, or learn, and seriously take action, I'll be willing to bet that the positive feeling that will follow by spending time on it will persuade you to want to do more and more on your list. Pretty soon you'll be spending your time on what you want to do and learn about.
"Don't just survive life, live it, experience it, and learn from it."

9. Personal Time/Meditation- Always take the time to emotionally recharge your internal battery of life, and reflect on your thoughts and actions in life. Clear the mind of troubled thoughts, seek understanding in your challenges, and find inner peace.

Similar to "self improvement," which focuses on taking the time for the expansion of who you are and who you want to become, personal time carries even more weight as to how important it is to live a successful and happy life that doesn't lead to burn out or loneliness, or worse…both. Personal time, or meditation, is taking some quiet time for yourself so you can clear your mind by sorting through your emotions and thoughts, emotionally recharge, and find meaning and understanding behind your thoughts and actions.

We spend so much time earning a living, or perhaps just trying to financially survive, or trying to keep everyone happy around us (professionally and personally), that we forget to take a timeout for ourselves to sort through our thoughts, to seek the meaning behind our lives, and make corrections where needed, simply because we don't stop moving long enough to address our own thoughts.

By taking time to meditate or simply listen to some music and reflect on your thoughts, this allows you to be more in control of your emotions so your emotions don't control you. It gives you the time you need to truly reflect and contemplate on your thoughts and life itself by spending time alone to search for the understanding and meaning behind the moments in your life. Clear the mind of unwanted thoughts or negative emotions, and ultimately finding inner peace with topics that are troubling you.

There are many ways to take a timeout away from the world and emotionally unwind our thoughts and quiet the mind. Meditation is one of the greatest ways to quiet the mind, and there are several forms and ways to mediate, but the overall key is to spend time sorting through your thoughts, letting them go one by one as they come to the surface of the mind, and ultimately emptying the mind to reach a level of peace and joy within. Similar to cleaning an email inbox out, the goal is to reach a level in your mind that you're no longer thinking about any one thought and allowing your mind to drift with your breath and have no other thoughts plaguing your mind with troubles and worries. You're setting your mind free and the feeling is rejuvenating, inspiring, and beautiful.

Moving meditation is another popular way to relax and reflect on life, because it's directing your energy and thoughts on the task at hand that brings enjoyment and offers personal time to reflect and clear the mind. Some examples of this would be gardening, woodworking, cooking, jogging, walking, or whatever brings a smile to your face when you do it, allowing you time to be alone with the task and your thoughts. This allows you time to clear your mind, and sort through thoughts and reflect. This is why having a hobby is so important and is healthy for the soul. Moving meditation is easy to do because you focus your mind on one thing, like gardening or hiking. You can forget about your worries and spend time in a state of bliss, and this will allow you to take on life with a more clear and focused mind. It offers a timeout from your burdens in life, even if it's just for a few minutes, and that's one of the keys to happiness. The overall idea is you're spending time doing something that brings joy to your heart and allows you time to reflect on thoughts and emotions and clear the mind until there is nothing left but the task at hand you're performing. Keep in mind some actions allow for more personal refection, while others demand more concentration for a simple timeout from life. As an example, riding a bike for 10 miles is a great escape and allows you time to sort through your thoughts while enjoying what you're doing. The second example is mountain biking. This demands more concentration on the action so you may not be able to sort through your thoughts, but it allows you an escape from your life's burdens to simply enjoy the task at hand.

"We cannot see the answer to a problem until we understand the meaning."

10. Positive Surroundings- Always try to surround yourself with positive people, a peaceful environment at home and work, and things that bring a smile to your day and energize your soul.

Our surroundings can have a strong influence on us including our motivation, energy level, and overall state of mind. Scientific studies have proven our surroundings affect us and are actually taken into great consideration when designing workspaces. Think about it, have you ever been in a room before and said how uncomfortable it was to be in the room? How about the opposite, have you been in a room before where you thought it was an incredibly relaxing environment? Look at fast food restaurant designs, some design layouts have planned right down to the chair design and temperature of the space to encourage us to eat and leave quickly for faster customer rotation. How about the weather? Ever notice how a sunny day or gloomy rainy afternoon affects your energy level or motivation? How about looking at the same broken item everyday and how it triggers the same negative thought every time you see it?

Everything in this physical universe is connected, and has a direct affect on everything else. The key is to identify what kind of energy you want out of a space or environment, and make the changes to create it. If you want your living room in your home to be a sanctuary of peace and relaxation, but every time you enter the room you notice a mess on the floor, a leg of the couch that's wiggling, a fish tank that needs drastic cleaning, or a stain on the carpet, then you really have a sanctuary of stress and not relaxation. By identifying what you want from a space (personal or work) and make the right changes, you will find yourself more relaxed and happy, or motivated and inspired, by the way you set up the environment in a space.

People also play an important role in the environment we create for ourselves. If you want to be more successful in your career, then you need to interact with successful people and let their knowledge and energy rub off on you. It's hard to propel forward in your career and ambitions if you don't interact with the kind of people that have succeeded, or have similar ambitions, compared to surrounding yourself with complainers about the work and how much they hate it.

Remember, **"You can only move forward if you're reaching forward."**

You also want to be aware of the negative people in your environment that affect you. We all have that person in our lives that swims in negativity, every story they share, every challenge they face is a hateful negative moment, it's like they're a magnet for negativity. You need to ask yourself why you continue to interact with this person and let them drag you down emotionally and sociologically. You need to make the choice of either helping them see the positive side of things instead of simply absorbing their negative views, or simply walk away. You have a choice what you consume, so make sure to be emotionally aware of your surroundings, how they affect you, and what you should be tuning into to propel you forward with positive thoughts, while tuning out the negative and not allowing it to affect your frame of mind. Change what you can in your work and personal environments, learn to accept the things you can't change, and I believe you will live each day with more happiness and inspiration with positive surroundings.

11. Life Purpose and Goals- To succeed, we need to have a goal or purpose in life, a direction. Discover your life purpose and goals, and you'll find your meaning in life.

It's hard to go for a ride in a car if you don't know where you're headed. Life is the same way, having a direction and destination provides you with meaning and purpose in everything you do. A person needs to take a moment of pause in life and truly decide what they want out of life and set personal goals. Otherwise, you'll find yourself like a sailboat with no sail, adrift at sea and at the mercy of the wind and water to direct you and decide where to send you. But if you decide to look for what you want out of life and what your life purpose is, then you can steer your boat in the direction your heart desires, and all your actions in life now have a direction and purpose.

Of course, along the journey we call life, things will happen that may inspire you to change course, but that's what makes life so beautiful. The key is life is not about the destination, it's about the journey, but you first must choose the destination to have a journey with purpose.

If you have a love or passion for something in life, I would encourage you to explore the options on how you can make it more a part of your life. Maybe it's sports, but that doesn't mean you have to be a professional ball player for it to be a part of your life. There are plenty of professions that surround baseball that could allow you to combine your talents with your passion. Maybe you love photography, you could get into sports photography, or if you're great at writing, why not look at becoming a sports columnist. Maybe you're already set in a career in life you love, but this is a second love in life, so how about teaching little league to kids, or playing adult softball. You see, there are many options a person could consider to follow their passions in life, but it's up to you to make it a part of your life.

Maybe you discover your life's goal is to help people, but you still want to continue with your current career, so why not spend your spare time helping organize fundraisers for food drives in your home town. The possibilities are endless, but you have to not only have passion in life, but also choose the purpose and goal within that topic, and then take action and make it a part of your life before it becomes one of those "I wish I would have" stories.

There are many ways to live your passion and purpose in life, so find your purpose and your life's goal you seek, steer the boat, and the wind will come.

12. Live to Give- A true legacy is not what you've accomplished in life for yourself, but what you have done for others. Bringing joy, helping others, and touching lives can bring the greatest moments in a person's life and bring true fulfillment in the heart.

The key is to live a life with fulfillment and meaning, so you need to apply yourself and your talents to help others. Self accomplishments and glory mean nothing if they don't touch and inspire others along the way, without it our lives have little meaning.

The world is an amazing and beautiful place to live, but also challenging on many levels. We can easily get wrapped up in our own problems or interests in pursuit of our own goals, and forget about helping our fellow man. The truth is helping one another is at times even more important than helping ourselves, and indirectly gives us just what we need, because helping others can be one of the greatest joys in life. That's really the underlining goal of all our thoughts and actions, which is finding joy in our own life.

We are all connected and what affects one person, can affect all of us, and that's why we have to help one another and grow together. If one of our main focuses in life was to help each other succeed, there would be little need for war, greed, anger, or hate. Think about it, the top of the mountain can be a lonely place if you make it there by yourself, but to help others reach the top of the mountain will give you more fulfillment then if you made it there by yourself. You are now a part of the other person's life you touched and helped up that mountain side, and that's a beautiful view, better than 100 mountain tops alone.

To live a positive and fulfilling life, you should make it a quest to find a way to help others through your journey in life and what you do, because there is no greater feeling than helping your fellow man. Perhaps it's simply mentoring a new coworker to be more successful and learn the traits to succeed in their new role. Maybe it's spending more time helping your son with his curve ball for baseball, instead of saying, "I'm too busy with my own things right now."

To summarize, here are the 12 key elements for success and happiness. Remember to incorporate them into your life, and you too can live the life you choose to live.

12 Key Elements for Success and Happiness!

1. **Thoughts are Things-** Everything starts with a thought. What we believe, think, and envision in our mind is the beginning to our actions and reality we choose to live in.
2. **Responsibility-** Acceptance and taking responsibility empowers you to take control of your life.
3. **Compassion-** All actions, thoughts, and words in one's life should be driven by compassion, pride, and joy.
4. **Laughter-** See the joy in every moment life brings you and express your happiness with laughter and smiles to live a life filled with joy.
5. **Gratitude-** Always be grateful. Gratitude leads to joy and peace of mind, allowing you to be free from the burdens of the wants and needs of life.
6. **Optimism-** Always be optimistic no matter what challenges you face. Optimism will allow you to see beyond a problem to find the benefits of any moment.
7. **Believe-** To truly be happy and successful in life, you need to have faith and believe! Believe in yourself, in others, and in life itself.
8. **Self Improvement-** Life is about self improvement, mentally, physically, and spiritually. To love yourself, you need to take care of yourself, challenge yourself, and keep growing.
9. **Personal Time/Meditation-** Always take time to emotionally recharge your internal battery of life, and reflect on your thoughts and actions in life. Clear the mind of troubled thoughts, seek understanding in your challenges, and find inner peace.

10. **Positive Surroundings-** Always try to surround yourself with positive people, a peaceful environment at home and work, and things that bring a smile to your day and energize your soul.
11. **Life Purpose and Goals-** To succeed, we need to have a goal or purpose in life, a direction. Discover your life purpose and goals, and you'll find the meaning in life.
12. **Live To Give-** A true legacy is not what you've accomplished in life for yourself, but what you have done for others. Bringing joy, helping others, and touching lives can bring the greatest moments in a person's life and bring true fulfillment in the heart.

Remember, "Life is not about finding yourself, it's about creating yourself."

Chapter V
Transforming Positive Thought to a Positive Life

V. Transforming Positive Thought to a Positive Life

"Happiness and enjoyment of life comes not from what you have or don't have, it's your perspective of life itself." Having a positive mind and a positive attitude toward life can lead to a joyful, successful, and fulfilling life. The challenge is it's one thing to recognize the importance of it, and it's another to figure out how to adjust your way of thinking to enjoy life, no matter what life brings your way. Have you ever had a friend or witnessed a person that seemed to have everything they wanted in life, but they had very little happiness in the life they live? How about a person that's going through some amazing struggles in life, maybe it's serious money issues, job problems, major health concerns, family or marital issues, or even the loss of a loved one. Yet no matter how much challenge they had to take on in life they found a way to be happy and see the silver lining of their life. "It's not about what you have or don't have, it's your perspective on life itself." I'm talking about the power of positive thinking.

The key is to become more emotionally aware of ourselves and spend time focusing on what we really care about in life. Utilizing positive thought fueled with love, compassion, gratitude, belief, and self improvement, to drive our actions and spend less thought and energy on what we don't want in life. By training our mind to always be looking for the good in every moment or lesson in life, we can find peace, understanding, and happiness no matter what. This is exactly what takes a person from suicidal to community leader, from bad husband and father to loving husband and dad, or a person on a losing streak in life to concurring the life they want personally, physically, financially, and spiritually.

Here are 5 empowering exercises you can do to help you refocus and train your mind on what is important in your life. It includes things to do on a daily basis to make them a part of your life to get the greatest fulfillment and joy in every day, by taking positive thinking and turning it into a positive life.

5 Empowering exercises to transform positive thought to a positive life.

1. Gratitude and Love List

It's difficult to be happy if you're spending most of your time thinking about what's troubling you, what's wrong today, what may go wrong, what you can't control, or when you get really frustrated finding yourself listing everything that's gone wrong in your life. I know, I'm also guilty of waking up and immediately thinking of the challenges I had to face for the day and sorted through several negative thoughts about why I didn't want to go to work and face the day, versus looking at the positive side of things by thinking of reasons why I want to wake up and greet the day and go to work.

If you really want to enjoy life to its fullest, and have a life filled with joy, then you need to focus on what you're grateful for and love in your life. It sounds easy, but truthfully have you ever sat down and given it some thought about what really matters in your life and what you're truly grateful for? Sure, anyone can say with a quick response, "I love and care for my spouse and children, parents, dog, friends, and health." But I'm talking about taking yourself beyond the obvious. I encourage you to take the time now and use the following blank 2 pages to challenge yourself by spending the next 15 minutes to rediscover everything you're grateful for and love in life. I made the 2 lists side by side so you can copy the pages to keep. I would encourage you to copy the lists and put it somewhere you can read it once in a while to remind you of what's important in your heart. Keep in mind the longer the list, the more things you'll discover you love in your life and are grateful for, because it's easy to list a few obvious items but we need to look deeper and longer into our soul.

As an example, here are some things that I'm personally grateful for and love in my life, to give you an idea of what I'm suggesting to think about when you make your list to expand your mind beyond the obvious.

EXAMPLES:
What I'm grateful for in life:
I'm grateful for……..
- *Having a loving wife and 3 amazing kids.*
- *Having a great and safe place to call home.*
- *To have a boat to spend family time on the water and enjoy life doing my favorite hobby.*
- *To have so much family to lean on and spend time with in life.*
- *Having 2 wonderful Siberian Huskies that give me and my family unconditional love.*
- *The challenges I'm faced with in life to learn and evolve as a person.*
- *For all the people I've met or have been a part of my life (good and bad) to learn from them and become the best person I can be.*
- *Having asthma, the challenges that it has brought and the opportunities I may have never have noticed without having this disease.*
- *Failing so I can learn to succeed.*
- *Having a good job when some people struggle to find work to financially survive.*

EXAMPLES:
What I love in life:
I love………

- *My wife and kids with all my soul and being.*
- *The beauty of the world, with the serenity of the ocean, the color of nature, and the abundant variety of life in the animal kingdom of the planet.*
- *Making my wife and kids smile and laugh, which brings a special joy to my heart.*
- *The opportunity to face fear and failure so I can learn to overcome and triumph.*
- *That I can raise children and be a teacher and mentor of life for them.*
- *The amazing peace I feel looking at the waves of the clear Caribbean waters on white sandy beaches.*
- *Bearing witness to the lessons that nature can teach us on overcoming obstacle; from forests being reborn from the ashes of a forest fire to an orphaned pup of a wolf winning against all odds and living a great life.*
- *Looking at the stars on a clear night in awe and being reminded and inspired on just how vast our world and universe really is.*
- *Listening to music and getting lost in thought and emotion by the rhythm and poetry of a good song.*
- *Watching movies and falling deep into the storyline to be a part of another world or adventure as an escape from the here and now, and forgetting about today's worries, even if it's only for a couple of hours.*

I hope the examples help because it's your turn to make a list of your own. Remember, the more time you spend, the longer the list, which will have a greater impact on you as you remind yourself just how much you're grateful for and love your life.

What I'm grateful for in life:

I'm grateful for…

1.	
2.	
3.	
4.	
5.	
6.	
7.	
8.	
9.	
10.	
11.	
12.	
13.	
14.	
15.	
16.	
17.	
18.	
19.	
20.	

What I love in life:

I love…

1.	
2.	
3.	
4.	
5.	
6.	
7.	
8.	
9.	
10.	
11.	
12.	
13.	
14.	
15.	
16.	
17.	
18.	
19.	
20.	

2. Appreciating Work

We spend a major portion of our time in life working to make a living, and it can be easy to find ourselves dwelling on all the challenges and difficulties of the job. What's worse, is from time to time we lose sight of what we do enjoy about our work, our employer, and even the line of work we're in, when in the beginning you may have enjoyed it or even loved your work. I believe this is also one of the reasons why so many people today switch jobs so much, because they fail to see what they do enjoy about their current work situation and seek out something new to find that enjoyment again.

If you want to put more wind in your sails again and smile on your way to work tomorrow, I suggest trying this next exercise to redirect your thoughts on what you enjoy in your work.

Take 15 minutes and make a list of at least 20 things you enjoy about what you do for work, who you work for, and why you do it. To help you, I've made some examples to give you an idea of some of the areas you should be thinking about when making the list. I've also included the next page as a fill in sheet for your own list for convenience. Take the time now and remind yourself of the meaning behind your work and all the little things you enjoy about it.

EXAMPLES:
What I like about my work...
- *I like the fact that I get to work outdoors in my job with construction.*
- *I love that I only have a 10 minute commute to work every day.*
- *I like the idea that I work for a company that is considered a leader in the industry and helps make changes to how things are done to make a difference for the good.*
- *I'm proud of the company I work for because...*

- I have 2 great friends I get to work with all day long that makes work fun.
- With how demanding my job is, I really appreciate how flexible my new boss is in letting me leave work early for different reasons.
- It feels great to teach my skills to others, so I enjoy mentoring new hires to the company.
- When I think about the service our company provides, I enjoy what I do and the work we provide to help others.
- I'm not just a framer; I build houses for people to call home, so I put pride behind every timber I put in place and every nail I drive in.
- I love working with my hands to create things.
- My job has the perfect work hours for me so I still have the time I want with my family.
- I have a comfortable work environment with a good manager and great coworkers.

What I like about my work…

1.	
2.	
3.	
4.	
5.	
6.	
7.	
8.	
9.	
10.	
11.	
12.	
13.	
14.	
15.	
16.	
17.	
18.	
19.	
20.	

3. Start Each Day Smiling

Every morning without fail, the sun rises and a new day is upon us. But instead of greeting each day focusing on love, joy, and inspiration, the average person awakes and immediately starts thinking about all the reasons why they don't want to get up in the morning. Focusing on all the problems they'll have to face for that day and the difficulties it will bring. I know I've done it. We find ourselves too often awaking to the morning sun listing what we have to do and what problems we have to face, not to mention the common excuses of why you don't want to face the day, like I'm too tired, too sore, not feeling well, unmotivated, you name it. So my question to you is this: How do you have a successful and happy day if you only look at the reasons not to get up, and view everything you have to face in life that day in a negative light? The answer is change! Change your perspective on the day before you even start it. By adjusting your perspective of the day from the beginning, it will have rippling effects to your entire day because of what you choose to focus on and how you choose to see it. As they say, "Don't wake up on the wrong side of the bed."

It's as simple as a choice, to either think about what you don't like about your day, or what you appreciate and look forward to for the day. If done right, you will feel more energized and inspired to take on the new day because you're focusing on what's great about the day and life itself. Even the challenges you have to face that day can be viewed as either a problem that has to be battled, or as a learning experience to evolve from. We all have our challenges in life, some greater than others. Maybe you're facing a never-ending battle with a weight problem, or not getting along with your spouse, or are dealing with serious financial problems. But you know that no matter what your problem is, there's someone else out there dealing with an even greater challenge, like the loss of a loved one, maybe a child, or a battle against a terminal disease, or fighting starvation in a poverty stricken region of a 3rd world country. What I'm saying is, life is never as bad as it could be and you still have a choice to stand tall and embrace the day with everything in your heart, or give up on the day before it's even begun, working through the day with anger, hate, and frustration in your heart. The choice is yours.

Here's an exercise to try starting tomorrow morning. As soon as you wake up, be aware of your thoughts and do NOT allow yourself to think about the negative side of what you need to accomplish that day. What you want to do is think about what you look forward to for the day, and the reasons to be happy and joyful. If you're unemployed, be happy you still have your health to seek employment. If you're dealing with a never-ending battle against weight loss, think about what makes you smile in life and find what motivates you and lights up your heart to keep trying to lose the weight.

Simply open your eyes, smile, and think of a few reasons to look forward to and love today. The easiest way to start this powerful morning habit is to have your own way of greeting the day, having it prewritten to recite to yourself as you're waking up to greet each day with inspiration, and then list one or two reasons to add for the day to look forward to it. By doing this, you won't struggle on what to think about for the first few morning as you try and change your habit of your thought patterns when you wake up. You're basically creating a morning affirmation that changes a little for each new day.

Here's an example: *It's a brand new day, I love my life and my family and today is going to be a great day! I'm looking forward to getting to the new construction job site today and spending time working on building out the layout of something new. I really love what I do because I get to work outside and build and create things, how cool is that.*

After awhile it will become a habit to awaken with a smile and think only good things about today. Start by writing a sentence or two that works for you and fill in a couple of things that makes you engage in that day, to motivate and inspire you to take on the day with joy in your heart. Remember, you tell the brain what reality you choose to see and live that day, and the body follows the brain's commands and you'll feel a difference emotional and physically. I'm talking about less stress and more energy and motivation, more interest and mental engagement in your work, and happiness in your heart.

4. Empowering Affirmations

"Happiness and enjoyment of life comes not from what you have or don't have, but your perception of life itself." It comes down to dedicating yourself to find the good in every moment and focusing your mind on the light, in even the darkest of moments. You need to teach yourself to direct your thoughts on what you want to accomplish in life and that you have the power to succeed and be happy no matter what the odds, and you can do this by using empowering affirmations. I'm talking about affirmations worded to inspire your drive to live life as you choose. By wording your affirmations in such a way that you're telling yourself who you are, what you're capable of, what the outcome will be, and by repeatedly telling yourself these things like "I can, I will," instead of "I'm not sure," or "I can't do this." Within words lies great power, and you have the ability to fail or succeed right from the beginning. You will help form the reality you choose to live in your mind, and when it's real in the mind, then you can make it a reality in the world.

In the next chapter we're going to discuss affirmations more in depth, and I'll share with you my top 10 tips for writing great affirmations for accomplishing your goals in life, which will help with writing your own empowering affirmations as well.

For a great empowering affirmation, you'll want to keep it simple so it's easy to remember to recite it to yourself throughout the day, and make it an inspiring affirmation that empowers you and is useful for any problems you come across for the day. Below are a few sample suggestions to get you started, along with an open area for you to write down some of your own ideas after reading through the examples to help you find one or two that fit your needs.

EXAMPLES:
- *I can do anything!*
- *I love life and who I am!*
- *I can, I will!*
- *I'm creative and brilliant!*
- *I love people and what I do!*
- *I am at peace, and love life!*
- *I will succeed!*
- *I believe!*
- *Have faith!*
- *Everything happens for a reason!*
- *The only limitation is my imagination!*

Time to write your own affirmations. Write a couple of empowering affirmations for yourself that you can use starting today and see the difference it can make as a daily reminder of what's important in your life.

---

5. Life Goal List

If you want to focus on what makes you happy in life, it helps to know what you want out of life and what your life goals are. Now it's one thing to know your direction in life for a career, or the level of financial strength you want to achieve, or how many kids you plan to have, but what about the more simple goals of what you want to experience out of life. Some may call this a "bucket list," which is a list of things you want to accomplish in life before you die. Basically, you're creating a list of things you want to experience, see, and do throughout your life that will help you live and grow as a person. Sampling what life has to offer you and teach you by experiencing things you don't normally do. I've seen people change by walking through this exercise because creating a list helped them discover so many little things they wanted to see or do and have forgotten about, or worse, allowed opportunities to slip by leaving voids in their life. By creating the list, you are defining specific things you want to do or experience in life and it can be quite liberating to think about the things you want to try or accomplish in life someday.

The list can be as long as you want, and in fact the longer you can make it the more you're discovering what you want out of life. When you write out your list the easy ones will come first, but as you push yourself to think about what else you want to try, discover, or accomplish in life, it becomes a journey into how you want to evolve as a person. Because with every experience you want to try there is a reason behind it. Maybe it's a fear of heights you overcome by skydiving, or try writing a book because you've always wanted to see if you had it in you. As an example, on my life goal list I had ice sculpting. I once saw a TV show about an ice sculpting competition and I was amazed on how a person could take a simple block of ice and turn it into a one of a kind piece of art, and I wanted to try that. I wanted to experience what it would be like to take something like a block of ice and chip away until I created something beautiful within it. So I put it on my life goal list to try ice sculpting someday.

I'm happy to say I can cross this off my list and it was fun to try. My 3 kids and I got ourselves a block of ice (which we froze in a simple bucket), took some wood chisels and a hammer and tried our hand at ice sculpting. It wasn't pretty, it was clearly much harder than we thought and the end result was a pile of ice cubes, but it was fun to try. If this was a bigger goal of mine, then I would keep working at it in hopes of discovering a new hobby. For me, I just wanted to sample the experience, not master the art of ice sculpting. But you never know, this is how we find new loves in our life, by sampling what life has to offer us and see how much of an interest it creates within us.

Here are a few keys to having an effective Life Goal List:
Key 1- You should keep it somewhere you can see it periodically so it stays on the front of your mind to remind yourself what your goals are. As time goes on, not only will you find the excitement of checking something off as completed on your list, you will also experience the feeling of "I did it." You will also find yourself adding things from time to time as new ideas are born from other experiences in life.

Key 2- No matter how big or small it is, impossible or improbable, put it on your list. The power of the subconscious mind is an amazing thing, and the list becomes imbedded in your subconscious by telling yourself, "this is what I want in life." And your mind (like a computer) will continue to work on what it needs to accomplish them. As an example, if you decided today you always wanted to buy a Chevy pickup truck, you're going to start noticing sales and advertisements for trucks for sale that have always been around you. Your mind never gave it any attention before because you never mentally gave it a defined priority in your life. Let's say you had "hot air balloon ride" on your list. When your spouse asks what you want to do for your birthday this year, instead of drawing a blank, you immediately think about going for a hot air balloon ride. This is because you have given this goal a priority in your mind and have chosen to remember it, because it was on the life goal list you look at once in a while.

Below are a few examples to give you an idea of some of the different categories of things to consider when you make your list. I've also added an open area for you to officially start making your own Life Goal List, and with the samples on one page and the blank page on the other; you can use these ideas to make your own first official list.

EXAMPLES:
1. *Try ice sculpting*
2. *Ride in a hot air balloon*
3. *Save a person's life*
4. *Meet the President of the United States*
5. *Meet the Dali Lama*
6. *Pet a lion*
7. *Ride in a limo*
8. *Fly in a glider plane*
9. *Visit the Great Pyramids of Egypt*
10. *Be on TV*
11. *Swim in the ocean*
12. *Lose 40 pounds and keep it off*
13. *Help a stranger*
14. *Witness something awe inspiring and breathtaking*
15. *Visit outer space*
16. *Witness a miracle*
17. *See an angel*
18. *Swim with a dolphin*
19. *Read one book a month*

20. Become a great gardener
21. Volunteer my time in a local nonprofit organization
22. Learn yoga
23. Help out a good cause in my community
24. Help kids read
25. Help out in an animal rescue shelter

Life Goal List   Done

#		
1.		
2.		
3.		
4.		
5.		
6.		
7.		
8.		
9.		
10.		
11.		
12.		
13.		
14.		
15.		
16.		
17.		
18.		
19.		
20.		
21.		

Chapter VI
Affirmations for Motivation and Success

VI. Affirmations for Motivation and Success

The use of affirmations is a powerful tool and method to not only define what you want in life, but also to help you achieve your dreams, goals, or simply live a life of peace and happiness. Adjusting your outlook on life is defining how you want to see the world or what you want to achieve. It helps create the internal spark of self motivation, inspiration, and conviction from within to drive a person's actions, and converts thoughts into the reality they choose to achieve or accomplish in life.

It's one thing to have an idea of what you want in life, to have a personal goal or dream, perhaps an ambitious business goal, but if you can't define it in a way that spells out exactly what you want for an outcome, it's going to be difficult to achieve. Simply put, if you don't know what you want, how are you going to achieve it?

Do you think an Olympic gold medalist only thought of their routine day by day, or do you suppose they envisioned themselves standing on the podium with the gold medal around their neck? They probably told themselves daily, "I can do this, I will be the greatest the world has ever seen, and I will win the gold medal."

By defining and affirming to yourself in present tense what you want and expect as an outcome, you're now focusing your thoughts, actions, and even your subconscious thoughts on your goal, which will help discover the steps that need to happen to achieve that goal. It doesn't matter if it's the Olympic gold medal, or simply losing weight.

Repetition of your affirmation is also key, because it will create belief in yourself and that you can achieve your goal. Belief is the magic ingredient that creates conviction within yourself to make your goals and dreams a reality. If done first in your mind, it will happen if you want it to take place in the physical world. Let's face it, you don't win an Olympic gold medal by accident, or wake up one morning weighing 40 pounds lighter.

The great secret of success is it really comes down to how you mentally take on your goal in life. It has a powerful bearing on the ultimate outcome. It's easy to get lost in thoughts of despair, doubt, or potential failure, with the overwhelming heights we may have to climb to make a goal a reality. Whether you're talking about battling breast cancer, or the challenge of quitting smoking, what we should be doing is focusing our thoughts on what we want, and not what we don't want or fear.

Think of an affirmation as envisioning and telling yourself what WILL be the end result. The result you want and have chosen. By doing so, you're creating internal motivation and inspiration that will allow you to see the opportunities necessary to make your goal come true, versus noticing all the obstacles that keep standing in your way.

Affirmations don't have to be reserved for your big dreams in life, you can use them for anything you want to change or improve. Examples can be about improving daily motivation, weight loss, boosting self confidence for dating, strengthening your bond with your family, quit smoking, overcoming a fear, overcoming a debilitating injury, reenergizing your love for life, or igniting the flame between you and your spouse. You can also use affirmations to remind yourself what's most important to you. Here is an affirmation example; "I love my kids, I am the greatest father in their eyes, and I give my undivided attention to them, they are my greatest treasures in life."

Whatever is important to you to achieve, you can use an affirmation to make it happen.

A great way to start is to define the problem in your life, determine the goal you want to achieve, and then write an affirmation that directs your thoughts in a manner that focuses on the outcome.

When writing an affirmation, the most important thing to remember is the wording you choose. Small changes to the wording can make a world of difference in the effectiveness. I had a friend of mine, Chris, that came to me awhile back and we were talking about his challenge with losing weight. He told me the affirmation he was using daily was "I will lose 30 pounds in 4 months and no longer feel heavy and out of energy." I told Chris this was a great goal, but not the best thing to be reminding yourself daily. Chris says, "What do you mean? I'm focusing on my weight problem daily and specifically what I want to achieve." So I told him to write down what he just said and look at what he's really focusing his mind on. This is certainly a great goal, but look at what you're reminding yourself of every day, an extra 30 pounds and you currently feel heavy and out of energy. What you want to do is focus on the outcome, and not the problem, and put it in present tense to tell yourself this is what is happening and to focus on what needs to fall in place to make the thoughts a reality. So I told Chris, try this affirmation and see what kind of results you get; "I'm much slimmer and lighter today, I feel great, I'm looking good, and have lots of energy." I touched base with Chris a couple of times over the next 3 months and, you guessed it, he lost 34 pounds over the course of about 16 weeks and was very happy and proud of his accomplishment. Chris said, "I took the affirmation you suggested and hung it up on my bathroom mirror so I would remember to recite it every morning and evening to remind me of what I expect from myself. It helped me focus on my diet and those long walks I was taking, and I am feeling positive about it." The power of thought has an influence on the body, including affecting the metabolism, and scientists contribute depression to weight problems because it not only affects your eating habits, but also the chemical makeup of the body. So bottom line is "mind over matter."

Affirmations can be utilized for anything that's important in your life you want to achieve or focus your energy on. Wording is key to creating a powerful affirmation, so here are my top 10 tips for writing effective and powerful affirmations.

Top 10 tips for writing effective and powerful affirmations.

10. Make it personal- Affirmations are best used as a personal motivational tool to direct yourself, your personal thoughts, and energy to achieve your goals in life.

9. Shorter the better- You want to make it brief and to the point so you can remember it and you want to recite it daily to yourself, but also long enough to have the detail needed to cover key elements of the goal outcome.

8. Involve action in your wording- By doing so you're focusing the mind and body to take action. Example, "I'm walking up to the podium as they give me a standing ovation and I take my award as Salesman of the Year."

7. Be as positive and inspiring as you can in your choice of words- Inspire yourself by choosing words that provoke you to take action and to do whatever it takes to make it happen by creating excitement for your goal.

6. Visualization- Keep a visualization of the goal you're affirming in your mind so you can frequently see your goal come true in the mind. Examples can be seeing yourself passing that finish line in first place, excepting that new promotion, seeing yourself after the weight loss, or perhaps meeting the love of your life. Visualization is a powerful element to bringing thoughts to reality by seeing it happen in your mind. Do you think a pro-golfer is daydreaming about the ball just missing the hole, or is he visualizing a perfect shot? You have to tell your mind and body what you first want before you can bring it to life. Seeing it come true first in your mind is key in defining to yourself what you want for an outcome. You can also use real pictures, like a photo of the house of your dreams, if that's the goal. Now you have an affirmation to recite to yourself and a photo to look at and keep in the front of your mind.

5. Use words that include your 5 senses- See, hear, feel, smell, and taste. By involving your senses in your descriptive affirmation, you're forcing the body to react with all its' senses and emotions, making it even more powerful of a reality in the mind. So every time you recite it, the body will feel as if it is really living that moment. As an example, if your affirmation is telling yourself and visualizing yourself walking up to receive the award you're aiming for, include in your mind hearing the cheers and applause.

4. Recite it daily, if not more- You should recite it daily to keep your goal at the front of your mind to attract the things you need to make it happen. It's also a great idea to hang a copy of it up somewhere so you can see it every day and recite it as often as you can, like on your bathroom mirror, on top of your dresser, or perhaps at your desk, in your car, in your wallet or purse, or even in your phone where you can view it whenever you want. The best suggestion is all of the above; surround yourself with your goal until you know it as well as your name. Another idea is to schedule an email or text to be delivered to yourself daily to force yourself to read it each and every day. If you use an electronic calendar for work, you can also schedule it to appear daily as a reminder to recite it again. Do whatever you can do to help keep it in the forefront of your mind.

3. Write it in present tense as if it has already come true- You want to convince yourself that it is happening now and not just tell yourself this is something you would like to achieve in the future as a hopeful outcome. A good example is stating, "I can breathe clearly now and the air has never been so refreshing." Compared to saying, "I want to quit smoking and breathe freely again." By presenting it in present tense, you're telling yourself "this is your reality," this is happening and it is real.

2. Focus on the outcome, and not the problem or challenge- You don't want to focus your thoughts on what's holding you back from your goal, you want to focus your wording of the affirmation on what you WILL achieve. By reciting it daily you're achieving it daily until it becomes reality. You want to tell yourself, "I'm financially stable and have plenty of money to pay my bills and live happy." Bad wording would be focusing on the problem, "I will not have money problems and debt collectors calling me." In this example, you're still focusing the mind on negative words like "money problems" and "debt collectors calling."

1. The number one tip- Believe- If you want your affirmation and goal to come true, you can't just read it, you need to believe it in your heart. When you're reciting it to yourself, you're also accepting it and believing in yourself. Feel the emotion and excitement as if it's happening right now. Let's face it, you can't fix a problem if you don't believe you can fix it. You can't achieve a goal unless you have faith in your ability to make it come true. Success starts with a thought, and if you don't believe in it yourself, then you've failed before you've even started. As I like to say, "The only limitations in life is our imagination."

"When your thoughts and intent are clear, your thoughts will become reality."

Here are some sample affirmations to use as a reference when you construct your own. These should give you an idea of how to incorporate the top 10 tips to build powerful and effective affirmations. Keep in mind when you write an affirmation for a goal, you have to create a compelling and believable outcome through your own words and visualization.

Remember, when you recite an affirmation like the samples below, you will want to add detail to encompass your senses, like what you hear and see. Use the wording to trigger a visual image of the moment and expand your thoughts to living that moment, so you hear the people cheering for you, you taste the victory in the air, and the feelings you have for accomplishing it as if it has already happened.

Sample Affirmations:
Quitting smoking- *I have strong healthy lungs that are clean and pure. I feel great, the air has never felt so refreshing to breathe and I have lots of energy.*
Losing weight- *I am much slimmer and lighter today, I feel great, I'm looking good, and have lots of energy.*
Achieving sales goals- *I'm standing in front of my peers accepting the Salesman of the Year award as they cheer me on for my accomplishment. I feel on top of the world with absolute happiness to have accomplished this.*
Family man- *I absolutely love my family! I'm full of joy and happiness as I spend time with my family, laughing, playing, and feeling ultimate joy and peace in my heart.*

Confidence builder- *I love the positive feelings of comfort as I'm in control and confident, feeling in charge of myself and my actions. People look at me with respect.*
Finance- *I am financially happy and money flows in my life.*
Dating- *I'm handsome, interesting, and secure; women notice my good looks and want to be a part of my life, and I feel excitement and bliss as my calendar is full of dates.*
Finance- *I'm feeling secure and strong as I balance my account and have lots of money.*

Remember to focus on the outcome and not the problem with your affirmations, and you'll soon find yourself spending more time, thoughts, and energy on what you want in life and how to make it happen, verses what problems you face and how they stand in your way of having a happy and fulfilling life.

Chapter VII
Defining Goals for Success

VII. Defining Goals for Success

You can't set sail across the vast ocean without a destination and compass to get you there. Life is the same, we need direction in our lives. Without direction, we're simply adrift in the ocean of life without a cause or purpose.

Defining your goals with a list of what you want to accomplish, provides you with the compass and destination in life. The next step is taking your list of goals to a more effective level. This strategy has been around for a long time, and they have taken on different names over the years, but they all follow the same principal. Some call it a vision board, focus board, goal board, and many others. The idea is you're listing your goals as a priority list by helping define exactly what's important to you, including your goals and dreams in life, by adding visuals and details to help make the goal as detailed as possible. This is like taking a detailed affirmation about an important goal and giving it life with a visual aid to define what you want, and it reminds you over and over again what you want out of life, so you never lose touch of your goals and dreams.

All too often I hear people talk about what they want to accomplish in life, but they never seem to give it any priority, always setting it aside to look into it at another time. Perhaps the excuse is not enough time, short on finances, don't have the resources right now, I'm simply too busy right now dealing with my current problems to focus on what I want, or they know what they want but they simply don't know how to achieve it so they set it aside in the long list of regrets in life.

One of our strongest senses we rely on is vision. By creating and using a focus board of images to display your goals and dreams to remind you of what you want to achieve in life, can act as a powerful visual aid. It acts as an emotionally inspiring and powerful tool for helping you focus on what's most important in our lives that you alone have chosen to focus on. By building a visual list of what's important in your life, it helps focus your energy, thoughts, and actions, acting as a constant reminder of what you want to achieve in life. Bottom line is you can't achieve a dream if you haven't decided on what you want to accomplish.

"The only limits in life are the limitations we give ourselves, just believe."

Take control of your life by building and using a vision board and determine what you want out of life. Put it down on paper, and make it clear to yourself where you're headed and what you want.

Vision boards are not just used for the big dreams. They can be used for anything that's important in your life you want to set as a goal for yourself. Examples include taking that dream vacation, buying the home you've always wanted, increasing your cash flow, learning how to play guitar, or getting that new job or career you've been searching for. How about that promotion you've been working towards, maybe it's buying the car or boat you've been wanting. Maybe it's simply things you'd like to focus more time on, like your family or spouse. How about personal improvement like getting back in shape, losing weight, quitting smoking, or to find a way to correct your injury and feel strong again. It can be about increasing the romance in your life, or your search for true love. Maybe you've always wanted to learn something new like yoga, scrapbooking, painting, or writing a children's book or romance novel. Perhaps your goal is to find a way to give back to the community, feed the homeless, or lend a helping hand to the struggling single mothers of your city. No matter what your goals are or how many you have, you can use a vision board to define them and focus your energy on what you consider important in your life and want to accomplish.

Creating a vision board is simple. It takes very little spending for supplies to put one together, just some quiet time to define your goals for yourself and a little arts and craft time to pull it all together. The time you spend creating your vision board can be an amazing process in itself, because you're starting to take charge of your life to live life on your terms. It can be electrifying to the soul, because you're spending time thinking about what you want to learn, succeed in, and care about. It offers the feeling of dipping yourself in the fountain of youth because it reenergizes the soul with new energy to take on the world. You are now defining what you really want in life and you're taking the time to focus on it. I've seen some people, including myself, say, "You know when you're making the right choices and are on the right path because you get a surge of positive energy that courses through your soul and veins that makes you feel good all over."

Keep in mind when you create your first vision board, it's not a once and done project, it's a living piece of art that connects you to your goals and dreams. The vision board will be a visual extension of your goals that will be ever changing as your wants, needs, and dreams change. As time goes on, you'll find yourself using it to help harness and focus your thoughts and energy on, just like a "Life Goal List" or affirmation for a goal, but you're taking it to the next level by having a visual definition to see every day and to remind you what's important in your heart.

Here are the steps and helpful tips for creating your first vision board to help you take the first big step of mastering your goals in life.

- **Decide on your goals-** Take some time to clear your mind and give it some thought as to what you really want in life, what your goals are, dreams, needs, and even wants in life. Do whatever you enjoy doing to relax and have time to do some deep thinking about this, maybe that's a long walk, sitting in your favorite spot in your home, listening to music, or perhaps some quiet time before you go to bed. What you want to do is come up with a list of your goals, define them with some detail, and then consider what words or visual aids you can use to help inspire yourself to focus on your goal. If you made a "Life Goal List" like we talked about in a previous chapter, this would be an excellent place to start for topics to use on your vision board.

- **Building the vision board-** To assemble a vision board you need to decide what you want to make it out of first. Typically this is an organized collage design with titles and visuals to summarize your goals. Here are the 4 easy steps to create your layout and design, and then we will discuss the different key components more in depth.
  - ➤ **Step 1-** Choose a backboard to use like foam board, card board, cork board, tag board, or perhaps a simple extra large piece of paper. Decide how large you want to make it. The amount of goals you have and where you want to hang it up, perhaps on the back of your bedroom door, will help you decide on the overall size.
  - ➤ **Step 2-** Choose visual images or pictures to summarize each goal. The closer the image resembles what you want to achieve, the better it is.
  - ➤ **Step 3-** Determine a summary of each goal. For example, "My dream home." Then add key details to better define the goal, like 3,000 square foot split level home, huge back yard with shade trees, move in date is summer 20XX.

> **Step 4**- Layout. Once you have your chosen goals, you can lay them out on the board or paper and determine a layout that creates the most emotional grabbing visual for you. Keep in mind, you don't have to use visuals for all your goals, you can simply draw in a box and define the goal in writing if you need to, but the visual aids are a key part to a vision board's success and can really help you by providing a picture in your mind of what you want.

- **Images and layout-** For the vision board to be effective, you want to find pictures and images that inspire and help you envision your goal in your mind with great detail to convince yourself this is truth, this is who you are not who you want to be, or this is my home not something I simply want, this is the reality I choose. If you're trying to lose weight, you may use a picture of yourself when you were younger. If your goal is to buy a new home, pick a picture that resembles exactly what you're looking for in the home. If you're inspired to write a children's book, try picking out a book that's the same style as you would like to write, then tape a piece of paper over the author's name and add your name as author. Take a picture of the book and use the image for your focus board. I knew someone that took a $1 bill and drew additional zeros on it to make it a symbol of $100,000 for her focus board. You can get creative to capture just the right image to help create that spark of inspiration you need on your focus board.

- **Where to get visuals-** The internet is a great resource for any kind of image you could possible want to print and use for your vision board by simply searching under key words for what you want. Other options to consider using are your own personal photos, post cards, or magazines. If you can't find a good picture to use, you can rely on your title line and 2 or 3 descriptive lines to detail your goal. It's ok if you don't have an image for every goal if you build good captive and descriptive text, but the images are ideal to go along with your description of the goal if possible.

- **Detail is key-** When you add your descriptive lines for the goal, remember to be specific. For example, if you want to lose weight, maybe you use a picture of yourself 10 years ago when you were slimmer. In the descriptive line don't just say, "I want to lose weight," define how much you will lose, like "I weigh only 170 pounds on March 1." This way, you're telling yourself exactly what you want. Did you also notice I put it in present tense? I did not say, "I will weigh only 170 pounds," I said, "I weigh only 170 pounds." You want to write the goal as if it has already been accomplished. Here is another example. Say your goal is to buy your first pickup truck. Along side of the new Chevy pickup truck picture you cut out from a car ad, you write, "This is my new red Chevy pickup truck with leather seats, V8 engine, upgraded rims, and tow package." The more detail you can add to goals that are important to point out, the more you will want to add it to the description. The more detail, the more real it becomes in your mind, but still keep it brief.

- **Time lines-** It helps to define a timeline for the goal if you can, it helps to create more priority and urgency, including at the subconscious level. We talked a little bit about writing the title and descriptions of the goal in present tense, but some call for placing you at a future time or event to get the full impact of the goal. This way, you have a specific target in mind and not just a someday in the future. You can also tie in the wording here from your affirmation, if you have one for this goal. Here is an example, suppose your goal is to get the next supervisor position at work, and you know they plan to fill one by the end of the year. Take a picture of the desk or office you would get when you get the position. If today is February 1 and you want to hit your goal as of December 31, then tell yourself, "Today is December 31 and I'm sitting in my chair in my new position as supervisor at work and I feel exceptionally happy and fulfilled."

- **Location of the board-** It's understandable that your vision board may be a personal thing, so you may want to keep that in mind when picking a location to hang it up in your home. Wherever you hang it up, you want to make sure to hang it somewhere you can see it daily, like your bedroom. The key is to have it in a good place so you can see it daily, and take the time to really focus on it for a couple of minutes each day. Ideally reviewing the vision board at the beginning of your day and just before you go to bed is most powerful. Perhaps you choose the back of your bedroom door or on top of your dresser. Reviewing your goals as part of your daily routine will help keep your goals on your mind and a priority in your thoughts. That's when you start seeing and recognizing the moments in your day that can help you reach your goals, because you keep reminding yourself daily how important these things are to you to complete, so your subconscious will continually be looking for opportunities to help solve it.

- **Keep it up-to-date-** A person's interests and goals can change over time as you work towards your goals, so it's natural that you may need to update your vision board. If one of your big goals is to purchase a new home, perhaps the home picture and detail you first picked is quite different compared to what you want now after house searching and discovering new features you didn't think of before, like you really want a two-story versus a one-story now. Keep your vision board up-to-date so your goals and visual images truly reflect what your heart desires.

Two key things to remember above all else is to make your vision board visually and emotionally inspiring to you. Secondly, keep it somewhere so you see it and read it daily until it becomes a part of you, and the dreams and goals will come true.

"One of the greatest secrets in life is there are no limitations in life except the ones we place on ourselves. Free your mind and live the life you choose."

Chapter VIII
Formula for Success in Life

VIII. Formula for Success in Life

We all want to conquer our dreams, goals, and ambitions in life, but success doesn't just happen. You have to dream it, believe it, and chase it if you really want it.

The real challenge we all face is how to obtain what we really want. Our perspective and approach is key to taking charge of our personal goals in life. Having the right frame of mind and looking at obstacles and problems as steps will help us get to where we want to be. This is instrumental in enjoying the journey verses fighting an uphill battle to success and achieving what your heart desires.

The approach can be equally as important and challenging. Every obstacle offers multiple solutions to overcome the problem. So what's the formula for success? What do we need in our action plan that will give us our greatest chances at achieving our goals and dreams in life?

If you're a mountain climber, you can't climb a mountain with just a smile and happy thoughts, you need a plan. You need to think about crucial steps to make it happen and make a successful climb or you're going to fall, and it can be a long way down. We need to think about things like: **Prep work:** What do you need to do to prepare for the climb? **What do you need:** What kind of gear do you need and what kind of problems may you run into? **Where do you start:** What rock face and approach are you going to choose to tackle for the climb? **Time line:** When are you going to attempt this climb? **Goal:** Is the top of the mountain our goal, or is it the first ledge at 250 feet up?

These are typical thoughts anyone would think of for a challenge you plan to face. But what are we really missing to give us our greatest chance at achieving our goal?

I believe if you want to achieve something great, you need a great plan. A person needs to take their planning to a whole new level. You need an action plan with a formula for success. Whether you're planning for a rock climb, your next diet routine, or an in-depth business plan to take your company to the next level, you need to reach deeper than just a to-do list. You need to put your heart and soul into your goals by asking yourself questions like, "Why do I want to achieve this?" "What if I don't achieve this?" "Do I believe in my heart I can do this, or will I second guess myself every day?"

I believe when you put your heart into something you really want, then anything is possible and you won't let anything stand in your way to reach your goals and dreams. Now to truly dip yourself into the waters of success, you need to understand some of the key components that are frequently missing from a person's action plan in life.

Have you ever known someone that was given every opportunity they needed to succeed at their goal, and they still failed to achieve it? Or how about someone that seemed to have everything they needed (money, resources, focus, and ambition) but they just couldn't achieve it? They couldn't get that side company off the ground, or lose those 30 pounds of weight, or figure out how to reinvent themselves and start that new career they kept talking about.

The reason why some people will fail while others will succeed is because of their determination and devotion from within for what they truly desire. This will allow them to take a step forward, when others take a step back, and allow the goal to become a part of them and who they are and not something on a to-do list. There is a formula of key components to achieving success, to take you from chasing your goals and dreams to living them. Any successful entrepreneur or athlete will tell you, if you want to stand on top of the mountain of success, the components of this formula are the keys to success.

Formula for Success in Life:

Dream & Purpose + Defined Meaning + Believe + Plan + Serve + Achieve = Success

Dream & Purpose- Every goal or ambition in life starts with a thought, a dream. To achieve that dream, you need to really envision what you want in life, why you want to accomplish it, and the purpose. This turns dreams into tangible goals in your mind first, then we can work on making it a reality. Every great idea or accomplishment in life starts with a thought or dream. When we were children, we naturally day-dreamed of what we wanted to be when we grew up; a major league baseball player, an astronaut, the world's greatest ballerina, the next big movie star or rock star, you name it. As grownups we forget to dream big because we see all the challenges and obstacles that have to be overcome to achieve that dream. Too often we find ourselves letting the winds of the world blow us in whatever direction seems right, because we don't take the time to focus on what we really want out of our life. We need to hold on to our dreams and continue to head the direction we need to, no matter what storms stand in our path.

In today's age, the children of America are too often raised to be exceptionally careful and over-parented, which causes a person to fear risk, change, and taking chances, because we focus too much on what could go wrong verses what could go right. How do we achieve that next great idea, or new invention, or try attempting something new that deep down your heart desires, if we focus on playing it safe and not take any risks. One expression sums it up best, "**Aim for the stars and you may hit the moon.**"

Scientific studies are now proving that it's our own mind that has the ultimate influence on what we can or cannot do, and not the outside world around us. The mind is a powerful thing, but too often enough we rely on outside opinion of whether we can accomplish something or not. Studies are showing that our own thoughts are far more influencing then the outside influence of others and the world around us. This means only you can truly tell your mind and body if something is possible. If famous martial artist and movie actor Bruce Lee would have listened to the doctors when he broke his back, he may have stayed in a wheelchair for life. Instead, he chose to ignore the outside world and believe that he had the power and the ability within him to walk again, and he did.

If you really want to take that next step in life or in your career for what you really want out of life, then you need to take the time to know what you really want. You need to dream it, and envision it with your mind. The second key to dreaming is to dream with purpose and understand why you want it. <u>There needs to be a purpose and reason for pursuing a dream to truly devote your heart to it</u>. Connect your goal or dream to your life and the impact it will make. As an example, let's say you want to lose weight and maybe you have a love for the outdoors and hiking, so use that to be the fuel for your dream. You now have a purpose to want to lose that extra weight, because the extra body weight is preventing you from enjoying your passion for the outdoors.

Maybe you dream of a day you no longer need a cigarette. Maybe your love for your grandchildren gives you a new reason and purpose to turn that dream into a reality with your newly defined motivation and purpose for quitting.

Maybe you have a strong desire and dream to help others, but you never knew how. Find the purpose and meaning behind your dream or goal, and you will have a self-sustaining energy source of drive and motivation that's capable of leaping over any obstacles that may stand in your way to achieving what your heart desires. That's the key; you need to desire it with your heart with purpose, and that will give you the power to succeed against all odds.

Defined Meaning- If you know what you want, you need to define it as clear as you can to yourself. The easy part is deciding what you would like to accomplish in life and finding reasons and the purpose of why you want to accomplish them, whether it's personal improvement like your health, or goals in business, or other side interests. The challenge to moving forward with your goals or dreams is to take your thoughts and define it at a level that it becomes clear and measurable to you, so you can then plan how to accomplish it.

If you want to lose weight, you need to be specific with yourself. For example, *"I want to lose 15 pounds in the next 6 weeks with a goal of losing 2-3 pounds a week and I will walk 2 miles a day and start my diet program today."* The clearer you can define your goals and dreams, the easier it will be to take action and make it happen. You can also make a list of all the reasons why you want to achieve this goal, as an exercise to help focus on how important this goal or dream is to you. This will help you commit to your goal or dream without reservation, because you have made it clear to yourself why it is so important to you, and defined it with what exactly you want. Let's say your goal is to stop renting and finally buy your first house to call home. Your goal is to buy a house, but how can you financial plan for it if you haven't defined exactly what you want, how much you want to spend, or what city to live in? You can't plan for it if you don't know exactly what you want. Your goal should be more like this, *"I will own a one-story ranch home with 3 bedrooms, two bathrooms, oversized kitchen, and an amazing yard with shade trees in the city of Littleton, Colorado for the perfect price of $X."* You can add a lot more detail for a goal like this, but you get the picture I'm trying to paint here. Detail is key, and the more you define your goal or dream, the more it becomes a clear picture in your mind of what your heart desires.

Believe- To accomplish anything truly difficult in life you have to BELIEVE. How can a person succeed in something if they don't believe they have it within them to achieve it? Without belief, you'll never find yourself giving it your all because you've already decided you can't do it so why push forward when you run into challenges? Without belief, you've defeated yourself before you even began, because you didn't buy into your own dreams and believe in yourself.

Never stop believing in yourself. Belief allows you to make the impossible possible, it gives you the courage to take that step forward when the world pushes you back. Belief will help you see the optional paths around an obstacle, and not just the problem holding you down. It gives you the courage you need to move forward when you're surrounded by overwhelming challenges. Believing in yourself gives you the courage to find the resourcefulness within yourself to make your dreams come true, and not give up at the first sign of difficulty.

Without belief, you can't find your way to achieve your dreams, it's the magic within us that gives us the strength to overcome what most would say is impossible. It's the wind in our sails that carries us to make the impossible, possible. Some would say it's not a lack of belief that's getting in their way to achieving their goals, but a lack of resources, lack of money, etc. I say if you have the will, you have the power. Success is not about the resources, it's about the resourcefulness of the person that leads them to succeed where others fail, but you have to believe in yourself even when others don't.

"The only limits in life are the limitations we give ourselves. Just believe…"

Plan- "Build a staircase to your dreams and you'll reach them one step at a time." One of my favorite quotes I've written because it tunes into one of the keys to success. It means success does not come to us; we have to seek it out by building a staircase to our dreams one step at time until we reach the top.

To take action on what you want in life, you need to take the time to think it through, plan it out, and write it down. Knowing what you want in life is not enough, you need to plan how you're going to achieve it. Without a plan, you don't have a map on how to get there, just a destination, and that's not enough. As the saying goes, "If you fail to plan, you plan to fail."

To take charge of your goals and dreams, you need to create a written action plan and include the following key elements to create focus and understanding in what needs to be done to achieve success.

> **Mission Statement-** Define your goal or dream and your "Why Factor," which is the purpose driving you to accomplish this. The Why Factor is the differentiator and motivator for why you will succeed. This gives you the motivation behind your belief, because you have determined why you want to achieve this.

> **Objective(s)** - List out exactly what you plan to accomplish by listing the key objectives within your goal and use details to define it as clearly as possible to

yourself. If your goal is to be the greatest salesman in your company, then define it with an objective that lists how much you have to sell and by what date. If your goal is to build the most popular website in the market for people to use as a resource to rescue dogs in shelters in your state, then spell it out in your objectives. Perhaps add your goal of the number of dogs to be placed in a home as an objective, which acts as a measurable objective for the goal to be successful.

➢ **Set Goals-** If you want to get to the end of your destination, you have to create a map of sub-goals or points along the journey you must reach to get you there. Sometimes our ultimate goal or dream can seem unobtainable because it's so grand and far out of reach, but if you establish sub-goals along the way, then your end result doesn't seem so difficult to reach. Think about it, would you drive cross country on one tank of gas and without stopping along the way a few times to check the map? You need to have smaller goals in mind of how far you would like to drive for the next stretch of open road before you need to fill up with gas again or need to rest your eyes. Your destination doesn't seem as far away when you start focusing on the sub-points you have to achieve before accomplishing the ultimate goal. You wouldn't train for a marathon by running 15 miles a day without some body conditioning. You have to build up your stamina first. You learn to run 5 miles, then 10 miles, then 15 miles. Remember, **"Build a staircase to your dreams and you will reach them one step at a time."**

➢ **Timeline-** To reach your goals in life you need to define a timeline to accomplish them. With a timetable, you will subconsciously keep on task because you have a defined goal of time to accomplish your dream and the steps that will get you there. Without it, you will not devote as much attention to it as you should, and will allow other things to take priority because you didn't define it as a priority for yourself. By building out a timeline in your action plan, you are challenging yourself to take action and stay with it. In order to move forward, you need to command yourself to move forward, and you can't work towards a dream or goal if you allow it to be at the bottom of your priority list. A common remark I hear from most is, "I simply don't have the time." I always challenge them to redefine how important this goal is to you, and if it's important to you, then you'll make the time. That's why a timeline for your goal and the steps within your goal are crucial to making your goal a reality.

➤ **Action Steps-** No action plan is complete with just goals, objectives, and a timeline. You need to have the action steps you're going to take that will get you there. The action steps are the things you need to complete to accomplish the objectives and hit the goals. This is your to-do list to move forward, and take control of your goals and dreams and make them happen. If you plan to enter in the next local marathon, then you need to start building up your stamina to handle the long race. Your action step is to start planning on running each week and slowly increasing them in length to build up the stamina needed to successfully run in the long marathon. The action steps are simply the list of things you have to take action on to complete your objectives, which are necessary to reach your goal.

➤ **Live It-** If you really want to accomplish your dreams and goals in life, then you need to LIVE IT every day. You should have action steps for every day to keep your momentum going and your mind focused on what you want. You can use affirmations which can be a powerful tool to keep your motivation going by reciting exactly what you want to accomplish, by stating it in present tense as if you already achieved it. *"I'm standing at the award banquet hearing the cheers and looking at all my friends and family as I have accomplished my dream."*

Reciting an affirmation will keep you continually thinking about your goal, keeping it at the front of your mind, and not allowing it to slip down the priority list for a few days. If the goal is important enough for you, then you're thinking about it every day to keep your motivation alive. Try and take action on something every day to keep your momentum going to reach your goals. As an example, if you're writing your first book and you can only find time to write every other day, then maybe on your off days you spend 15 minutes brain storming, or gathering ideas for the next chapter while you're driving to work or perhaps reading a book while you go to sleep to generate ideas for your book. Bottom line is, there's always work to be done and if you want it bad enough then you need to make it a part of you, living it each day, and keep chipping away at it until you succeed.

Serve- In every dream or goal in life, you should always include how it can serve and help others. There is no greater feeling then helping others. If you really want to accomplish something great, always include the element of how you can help people with your dreams and goals.

Your approach to your goal is just as important as the goal itself. You don't want to be pushing people out of the way to get there. Reaching the top of a career or a magnificent accomplishment can be lonely if you don't have others to share it with. Always make it a priority to help others along the way to your destination, and you will find yourself building a pyramid of respect, love, and support, with others cheering for you and your goals by including them helping you reach your own goal.

Make your goal and accomplishments in life more than just for you, make it for others and how you can help people along the way, and you'll always succeed no matter what the outcome. This also ties into the "purpose" you defined for your goal. For example, seeing how your accomplishment can be a voice of inspiration against the impossible, or how your goal will help others when achieved. How about what you've learned along the way with your mistakes and obstacles you've overcome? Sharing your experiences can be instrumental to others trying to achieve their goals.

Not all of us are aiming to join the Coast Guard to save lives, which offers an obvious purpose behind the job, but it helps to define the purpose in your actions for the meaning in what you're doing and why. When you achieve your goal and you look back at what it took to get there, you'll see the journey was even more important than the goal to your life and who you have become, so helping others is key. This is a huge step forward to living a life of success and happiness because you added more meaning behind it.

Achieve- A key to achieving your goals and dreams is to convince yourself you will achieve it. Achieve your dreams daily through visualizing yourself obtaining it, believing it, and daily dedication of your thoughts, actions, and heart. If you can visualize yourself achieving your dreams, then you will focus your mind to notice and attract the things you need to accomplish your dreams. You can't achieve something if you never think about it. If you want to make your dream a reality, then it can't be a someday, it needs to be today and every day.

When you visualize yourself achieving your dream, remember to use all 5 senses. See it, feel it, hear it, smell it, and taste it. Make it as real as you can in your mind. This is what we call a visual affirmation. See yourself in the winners' circle or holding that award. Hear the people congratulating you. Smell the food and taste the champagne being poured at your congratulations dinner, and feel the great sensation and emotions you have in accomplishing it as if you're in the moment right now.

By visualizing yourself obtaining your dream daily, you're telling yourself it's already happening, it's happening right now. Which, in turn, generates daily belief that it will happen for you and you harness great internal motivation to drive you towards what needs to be done to make it a reality.

By applying the formula for success to your goals and dreams in life, you can't go wrong. Pursuing your goals with your heart, defined conviction and meaning, belief and purpose, and with a plan of attack with all the key elements, you're destined to succeed at many levels. **"The only limitation in life is your imagination. Just believe."**

Chapter IX
Personal Time and Meditation

IX. Personal Time and Meditation

When we covered the "12 key elements for success and happiness," we talked about personal time and meditation and the importance of taking personal time for yourself to reflect on life and clear your conscious. We covered how important it was to always take the time to emotionally recharge your internal battery of life and reflect on your thoughts and actions. You need to take the time to clear the mind of troubled thoughts and seek understanding in your challenges to find inner peace. This can be accomplished by doing something you enjoy like a hobby, perhaps biking, walking, gardening, painting, or even chores around the home that hold your concentration for 15 minutes or longer, even like cutting the grass or washing the car. By living in the moment, you're putting yourself completely into it physically and mentally. You're allowing yourself a timeout from all the burdens in your life by simply focusing on one thing that you enjoy doing and setting yourself free from the burdens of life, even if it's just for a few minutes. During those few minutes, you're free. Free to lose yourself in the moment or action of the hobby, or to reflect on your life and sort through your thoughts and clear your mind. In some cases your hobby may demand enough attention to your actions, like mountain biking, that allow your mind to only focus on the task at hand, which allows you to step away from all your other thoughts, problems, and stress in life.

Meditation is similar, it's a process of sorting through a person's thoughts and also clearing the mind until you think of nothing else other than the breath you take moving in and out of your lungs, like the tide on a beach. If you do it well enough, it becomes a mental escape offering inner peace, clarity of thought and vision, and ultimate nirvana. Before we jump into how meditation works and the benefits of it, let's dive deeper into the need for personal time, and the challenges we face to living a life of peace and happiness.

The greatest challenge we all face is the stress of the thoughts and emotions that follow our problems in life. Maybe it's pain and suffering, or a broken heart, or maybe it's being over worked and still coming up financially short to pay the bills. Or maybe it's all the above. One thing's for sure is that everyone has stress in their lives, but the key is how you handle the stress and become emotionally aware of your feelings and the choices you make because of it. Sorrow or failure can cause a person to give up the fight, but it's an internal choice we make. The key is to take the time in life to clear your mind so you can think clearly and see the answers you seek and make the choices in life you want to make, which leads to a life of peace and happiness from within.

Some may say that in today's world we live in easier times, but I would challenge that notion because I believe we are consuming more personal stress than ever before. We find ourselves taking on so much in our lives in today's world, thanks to the advancements mankind has achieved over the past 100 years. We are moving at such a fast pace it's truly difficult to absorb what really matters in life, because time has become the most precious commodity in our fast paced society. The real problem is the average person does not take enough personal time or a timeout for themselves to simple think through their concerns, frustrations, or challenges, and spend time clearing the mind and thinking about what they truly appreciate in life to bring balance to themselves and have inner peace and happiness.

Another challenge we all face today is the amazing level of information we have access to. In today's world with its' rapid technology growth and burst in global communications, like the internet that reaches every corner of the planet and social media that can keep great masses of people in tune with what's happening in real time all over the world, we are simply overloaded with information and change. The average person is truly challenged to absorb so much knowledge and information and then balance it in your own thoughts and perspective.

The impressive increase of technology over the past few years allows a person to be in tune with all the greatest challenges the world faces on even a global scale, so everyone takes on the stress with situations that may be halfway around the world. 100 years ago, if there was a horrible accident leading to the death of a child in a town 50 miles away, you may never have heard about it. With today's technology, a story of a kidnapping or a couple sailing around the world 8,000 miles away, is heard all over the world through the news on the TV, internet, our smart phones, facebook, and twitter. You're going to hear about it and feel the emotions of the tragic story as you put yourself in their shoes and the stress that bears down on your heart. All this information, if absorbed in a negative light, can literally be toxic to your soul.

We all want to know what's happening in the world, from our own neighborhood to half way around the world, and for that reason today's global communications can be considered a beautiful thing. But the challenge is how do we handle so much stressful knowledge and news in our life besides our own personal daily stresses we face, like financial concerns or family problems. As the Prayer of Serenity says; *"God grant me the serenity to accept the things I cannot change, the courage to change the things I can, and the wisdom to know the difference."*

So the real question is: What do we do about all this stress in our life?

The answer is personal time and meditation. How we choose to accept things and eternalize them to a point of clearing the mind is the secret to managing our thoughts and emotions, or as I like to say, "being mindful" or "becoming emotionally aware" of our thoughts and actions and working through them. To do this, you need to take some personal time to work though your thoughts, and meditation is one of the greatest ways to accomplish this.

Meditation allows you to let go of your negative emotional burdens, by taking the time for quieting the mind. You can have clarity of thought which leads to an inner peace because you're taking the time for yourself to comb through your thoughts and emotions and clear the mind.

Meditation has been around for thousands of years. It's practiced around the world in almost every culture in some form or another. There are many reasons to adopt meditation and breathing exercises into your life, beyond dealing with daily stress and the search for inner peace. The medical industry has adapted it as a suggested technique to help lower stress, overcome fear, quit smoking or other compulsive habits, to lower blood pressure, and even for self healing. Meditation and breathing exercises have also been found to build stamina, increase vitality, strengthen the immune system, improve cardiovascular systems, respiratory systems, and the overall maintaining of a healthy mind and body.

Whatever your motivation is for considering learning meditation, you'll soon find it's benefits far reaching beyond your original motivation. **"To understand life and others, you must first know yourself; allow this to be a part of your journey in life."**

There are many styles and methods of meditation, and at first it can seem very difficult to do, especially in our fast paced society that has trained us to do twenty things at once. So to shut off your mind for a few minutes and let go of all those concerns and to-dos in your mind and just breathe, can be difficult at first, but when done correctly it's rejuvenating and refreshing, and I would encourage you to adapt it into your lifestyle.

Meditation is not as complicated as one would think. You don't have to sit in an uncomfortable position for hours chanting Sanskrit. It's really about bringing stillness to the mind, and there are some simple things to know to get you started.

In fact I would be willing to bet you're doing some form of "Moving Mediation" and you don't even realize it. Have you ever noticed when you're doing something you really enjoy doing like gardening, walking, biking, painting, sports, or whatever brings pleasure to you, when you spend time doing it you find yourself putting yourself completely into it? You focus all your thoughts into your actions and you are no longer dwelling on the stress in your life, and when you're done with your long bike ride, or gardening, you simply feel better. The reason is because you were focusing your mind on one thing, by living in the moment. You were spending time doing something you enjoy and not dwelling on all your problems. You may not have been clearing your mind completely and doing some form of meditative breathing, but for a short time you let go of your emotional burdens, enjoyed life, and allowed the noise in your head to calm, allowing you to see and think more clearly.

Having this be a part of your routine can play a big part in continually reenergizing you for life. I would encourage everyone to have something they enjoy doing that they can consider their "Moving Meditation," that allows them an escape from the needs of the world and gives them the opportunity to clear their mind, while doing something that relaxes them or brings a smile to their face.

Meditation has many styles and reasons for it's methods, but the basic principals are the same, and you can learn it by spending only a few minutes at a time. Here are some key items a person needs to know to get started.

Do I need a teacher to learn meditation?
If you want to get a coach for meditation, a class is going to be your best source. You can certainly self teach by diving into the vast world of the internet, there is an enormous amount of helpful information out there on the subject. Purchasing a book on the topic is also a good way to expand your knowledge on the different methods, and receive helpful detailed instruction to take a more devoted step toward learning meditation, beyond the basic introduction we will cover here.

How many different styles of meditation are there?
There are literally thousands of styles and forms of meditation and breathing exercises out there. Some techniques are specific in overcoming a problem, or to develop a specific psychological state of mind to focus a person's energy where it's needed. Other techniques are simply to empty the mind of unwanted negative thoughts. To narrow it down, I'll share 3 of the styles I've used over the years for a good place to start. But before we get to technique and style, let's cover some of the basics of mediation, and the typical questions you'll need answers to.

How do I sit?
Posture is important to allow for proper flow for your breathing and energy. Keeping your back straight is key with whatever position you choose. You want to be comfortable in your sitting position, but not so comfortable that you fall asleep while meditating. Ideally, you don't want to use any kind of back support like a chair if you can. Sitting on a pillow, on the floor, with your legs crossed is a very popular choice. If your body is not

capable of sitting on the floor, then a chair will do. Keep your head up but tilted slightly downward with a subtle happy facial expression. Eyes should be just slightly open which can help control the mind from wandering, but you may find this distracting and need to have them fully closed. The number one thing to remember about your posture and sitting position is to choose a position that will help you relax, but stay attentive.

How do you breathe while meditating?
You want to allow your breath to flow naturally and slowly in and out while allowing it to slow down with each breath, becoming deeper and more relaxed as if you were falling sleep. You're trying to bring your breathing and heart rate to a slow and calm state, while allowing the body's tension to drift away with each breath you take. You don't want to control or force the breath, but be mindful of it and slowly allow the breathing to become a natural, relaxed, deep slow breathing as if you were sleeping. Breathe in through your nose and exhale through your mouth. You can choose to exhale through the nose if it becomes more comfortable for you, but I believe the circle of air flowing in through the nose and out of the mouth creates a more circulating rhythm of air flow. Another key to breathing correctly is to breathe from the abdomen not the chest, allowing the breath in, to expand your abdomen outward and compress while exhaling. This is an important step, and it will be a different way of breathing than you're used to. Typically when you breathe in, your chest expands, but with meditative breathing you want to expand the abdomen (your stomach) when you breathe in and deflate as you exhale. After a while it will become very natural, but in the beginning it will be a learning process to be mindful of how you're breathing until you do it naturally.

How do you stop the random thoughts and clear the mind?
With one breath and thought at a time, you want to allow yourself to become relaxed but attentive. Allow yourself to focus only on the breath going in and out. As thoughts come into your mind, don't resist or fight them, but allow them to drift out as they came in without focusing or dwelling on them, always returning your attention to the breathing until there is only the breathing and no other thoughts.

How long do I meditate for?
I've found that the best method is to start out slow, only trying to meditate for 5 minutes at a time to start and working up to 15 minutes, then perhaps 30-45 minutes as an ideal goal. It's a good practice to have a goal in mind when you start for a minimal time to meditate. Then anything over that time is great because it can be discouraging to try, only to find you can't keep your mind still for even 60 seconds. You've got to have faith and take it slowly. It's common for this to be challenging, to control all those random thoughts coming in and out of your mind, so try not to be discouraged.

Here is an exercise you can use to start to train you mind not to wander. While in your chosen position, look at the second hand of a clock, and while slowly breathing in and out, apply all your attention to the ticking and moving of that second hand's movement, blocking all other thoughts out, and try this for 15 seconds. Once you can do 15 seconds without distraction, try 60 seconds. When you can do a full 60 seconds without losing your focus, try going back to trying a 5 minute meditation, focusing on your breath and no longer using the clock as a tool.

What should I expect?
To learn the art of meditation is simple once you know the basics. Bringing stillness to the mind is what takes time to learn, but if you're willing to put in the time, the effects and changes it can bring into your life mentally, spiritually, and physically, are absolutely priceless.

"The mind is like a window, the more you clean it, the better you can see beyond it."

It takes practice to learn to control the mind and all it's wandering thoughts. But with every few minutes you practice meditation, you'll discover the benefits with your nerves calming, your body relaxing, and your mind more clear and open.

I've talked with so many people that have told me they want to learn meditation, and have attempted to try it, but failed. They feel they can't even quiet the mind for a minute or two, so they will never be able to do it. It really comes down to dedicating yourself and finding the time to unplug from the world, even if it's only for a few minutes, to sort through your thoughts, clear the mind, and reenergize the soul.

To learn the art of meditation, I believe it also helps to have a purpose or a goal. Maybe it's to simply calm your daily nerves, create greater inner peace and see the joy in your life, or perhaps to overcome a compulsive addiction. Whatever motivates you to learn meditation, try it, because I believe everyone can benefit from it.

To help get you started, now that you know the basics of meditation, here are 3 techniques I've used over the years to (1) clear and still the mind for inner peace, (2) work through thoughts and emotions, and (3) reenergizing the soul with love and happiness.

1. <u>Meditating to clear and still the mind for inner peace</u>- The idea is to stop the mind from wandering through random thoughts and focus only on your breathing. The goal is to see and feel the energy and breathing of the body flowing in and out, allowing the mind to know nothing but the breath and energy of life. By focusing on the motion of the air circulating in and out, you can let go of your other thoughts. This is much harder than it sounds as our mind is actually a very busy and noisy place, and you'll naturally have thoughts and emotions drift through your mind. You need to resist focusing on these thoughts when they come into your mind. You need to allow them to drift away just as they drifted in, until you have emptied your mind. The more you practice this, the more you'll find it becoming easier to control your random thoughts and quiet the mind. You can set yourself free from all your burdens, concerns, and challenges in life, and simply breathe. Meditation is not about empting the mind to forget your problems, it's about calming the storm in your soul. You are controlling the amount of energy you place on the problems in life, and allowing yourself to take a step back from life for a few minutes and step forward with a clear, relaxed and focused state of mind, feeling refreshed and reenergized.

2. <u>Meditating to work through thoughts and emotions</u>- Once you can still the mind, then you have better clarity of thought, allowing you to focus or contemplate on one specific thought or emotion. This allows you to discover the true meaning it has to you, freeing your mind to make a decision on it once and for all. This is where you can clearly look inside yourself to find the answers you seek about yourself, life, and the challenges you face. It is here that I have actually written many of the reflections I've included in this book, as summaries of deep thought and contemplation of important things in life that I choose to dwell on to find understanding in. You'll find when you have a calm mind and

soul that it becomes easier to see the answers to problems you have, or find the meaning behind moments or challenges in life.

3. <u>Meditation for reenergizing the soul with love and happiness</u> - Once you have learned to empty the mind, you are free to see how beautiful life truly is. You can use this time to swim through these thoughts, which can be like drinking the elixir of life itself. Your mind is free to see beyond what your eyes can see, and look through life through heaven's eyes and see the beauty in all things and moments. It is here that you can focus on how much life means to you and what you appreciate and love about life that will illuminate your soul with energy, because you're focusing your thoughts with love for life. Most people spend hours a day consciously or subconsciously worrying about everything in life that's going wrong. But when you meditate, your give yourself the opportunity to rid yourself of all those worries and free your mind to spend a few minutes thinking about how much you love your spouse, children, family, friends, pets, nature, or life itself. Take the time to dwell on what brings joy to your life and the memories that make you smile.

We all want to live the best life we can. Through meditation you can clear and focus the mind to see and understand life better, to absorb more life than you ever thought possible, and live a life filled with love, peace, and happiness.

"You can't fill a cup which is already full, empty the cup and truly taste life."

Chapter X
Reflections and Quotes to Live By

X. Reflections and Quotes to Live By

We all want to succeed in life at some level or another. For some people they're looking for a successful relationship or wonderful family life with children and look at them as the joy and center of their universe. For others, they're in pursuit of financial success or launching a new company that rockets to greatness. For some it's simply being financially stable and having enough time and energy at the end of the day to make the kids smile and laugh. Some people live in very harsh and hostile conditions struggling for the right to live, while others live a safe but fast paced stress-filled life, but we all face the same universal questions in life: Why do I live the life I do? Why is life the way it is? Why is there so much pain and suffering in the world? Why did this happen to me? How can I succeed when the odds are stacked against me? How do I win a fight that can't be won? What is the meaning of life itself?

The key to understanding life is it can't be explained, it must be lived to find its purpose and true meaning to you from the lessons you'll experience along the way. I like to say,
 "We live to learn so we may learn to live."

The reflections I share with you here are not deep secrets of the universe, just simple truths of what you already know. They are reminders for you of what's important to be mindful of to absorb and understand life as much as you can along your journey in life. They're reminders of how to approach life to help you live the most rewarding and successful life you can, with no regrets or remorse, just simple inner peace and happiness with reflections and quotes to live by.

The quotes you find in this next chapter are reflections I've written over the years from my own summaries of life. As you read the quotes, take a moment of pause to reflect and contemplate on its meaning, and what it means to you. See if you can find a reflection that really speaks to you. Another suggestion is to post your favorite quotes on your cell phone or tape it up on your bathroom mirror to reach each morning, or perhaps hang in your workspace to offer a little daily inspiration so you can read it each and every day.

Reflections and Quotes to Live By

We live to learn so we can learn to live.

The meaning of life is not a way of life,
it's to live and learn from life itself.

Happiness is not a place or thing,
it's a state of mind.

To succeed you must first learn to fail,
and it's within our failures that
strength, courage, and determination are truly born.

When your thoughts and intent are clear,
your thoughts will become a reality.

With every challenge you always have a choice,
except it or change it,
but don't just complain about it.

One must always take time for reflection.
If you never look into the mirror, you will never see yourself.

Arguments, battles, and wars are the result from
untruths, greed, and fear.

Learn to clear the mind, listen to your inner self,
and speak the truth.
If we can master this, then there would be no need for war
at any level.

Surrender yourself to everything
and you will become everything,
from this comes understanding and truth.

Life is not a balance of give and take,
it's a balance of giving and receiving.

When your thoughts, words, and actions
are the same, your soul is in tune with who you are,
who you want to be, and who you will become.

You can't have triumph without struggles,
and it's within these struggles
that we can find ourself, define ourself, and truly live.

Life is about change,
become a part of the change
and make the world a better place.

Learn to have an open mind free of judgment
and you shall always find truth.

In life, find the purpose in every movement.

Go to a place within yourself where
there are no pictures and no sound,
and it is here you will find clarity of thought.

The search for balance is the search for peace.

The human soul is an ever changing creation
to be inspired and shaped by the challenges and lessons in life
and is capable of great divine evolution.

To understand life you must first know yourself,
for knowing others is knowledge but
to know yourself is true wisdom.
Allow this to be your journey in life.

The answers in life lie within us
because we are all truly enlightened.
We need only to slow down,
clear the mind, and listen to the heart.

We can never see past
what we don't understand.

The imperfections of life
is what makes life so beautiful.

Have faith in fate.

Happiness and enjoyment of life comes not from what you have or don't have, but your perception of life itself.

One of the most important things you can do for yourself is simply BELIEVE.

Sometimes our greatest accomplishments in life
are the lessons learned from our failures.

Courage is born in the presence of fear,
find the motivation from within to keep moving forward
and you'll prevail no matter what the outcome.

Do not allow your vision and happiness
to be blocked by judgment.
Put down your burden of judgment, it only imprisons you in
sorrow, blocking your vision of understanding.

Respect life and all living things
for we are all connected.

The beauty in life is not what you see
it's how you see it.

Sometimes it's not what we receive
but what we are denied in life
that propels us to succeed.

What weakens us can also strengthens us.
The challenges we face in life
are how we learn and evolve as people.
After all, what would life be like without our challenges?

Everything is ever changing,
bearing witness to this connection
gives understanding of the flow of life.
For every action, there is a reaction,
for every cause, there is an effect.

The future is not written in stone, but in sand.
Like a path in the forest, the path has been chosen,
but the curves in the path are ever changing
with choices you make,
defining the path itself by living it.

Don't lose yourself in the pursuit of success.
Mastering a skill set or earning lots of money will mean nothing
if you don't embrace life itself and seek meaning in your life.

Learn to see and feel with your heart and soul
not just with your eyes,
and you can experience things
you never thought possible.

You cannot control time, for time does not truly exist,
time is a countdown only from one perspective of space and
movement.

Peace can be found by understanding one another.

Is the snake evil for striking at you, causing you fear?
Or is it defending itself from fear of you?

Clear the waters of fear and you will find
understanding and tranquility with life.

All actions, thoughts, and words in a person's life
should be driven by compassion, honor, and joy.

In life, evolution is driven by the challenges faced.

It's the lion that gave the gazelle it's speed,
and the zebra it's stripes.
Everything affects everything.
The more we see this, the more we can change and evolve.

Love yourself
and the world will follow

Everything happens for a reason or purpose.
Learn to lay down your burden of why
and learn to accept what each moment brings
and what it teaches us.

To hold onto anger is easy,
to forgive is to be great.

To search for enlightenment one must
let go of negative thoughts, judgments, fears, and sorrows, and
surrender themselves to become a student of life,
freeing the mind to see life through heaven's eyes.

The only limitation in life is your imagination.

Do not hold onto regrets in life,
regrets only cause sorrow.
In life, things happen not by chance or coincidence
but for a reason.

Take heart in the journey at hand
and the path shall light the way.

Material things are not the root of happiness.
Happiness can only be found within.

Let go of the wants and needs in life and
learn to except and appreciate what life and fate brings.

Don't just live life, experience it, and learn from it.

Live and cherish each day as if there is no tomorrow.
For at the end of this life all that remains is
the memories and emotions experienced.

Let life take it's course, for what is, is.

Thoughts are things.

Within words (spoken or thoughts) lies power.

Everything is about choices.

What you experience and do in life
echoes into eternity.

Expect nothing and you will receive everything.
Give yourself completely to each moment in life and the life you live.

Science is great, mathematics and technology can do wonders, but to know yourself is true wisdom.

In life we are all teachers and students.

When you lose your way with a child or student, remember to view the challenges as lessons of life and to learn from each other.

When one loses their way
sometimes it's best to go back to the beginning
to find your way again.

We are never truly alone and lost, just confused.

The physical human bodies' ability
or mankind's advanced technologies,
cannot hold a candle to the strength
of the positive eternal energy of life
that lies within us.

Always look for the good in everyone and everything.

Dwelling on the negative emotions and hate in life
will give birth to new hate and negative energy in life.
Focus on the good and you will illuminate your life force
with the most powerful force in existence, LOVE.

Life is a gift, not a problem.
Embrace life with your heart and not your fists
and the world will respond.

Music is a doorway to our soul, speaking to our emotions and electrifying memories and thoughts of the past, present, and future.

To be open minded is to realize that there is no right or wrong, only opinion.

The mind of a child is a beautiful thing.
A human child is born with an innocent and open mind
like an unwritten book. They hold no perceptions of life,
and see things for what they are.
Children are not just the student but also our teacher.

One person can truly make a difference.
It only takes one to tip the balance of many.
Remember everything starts with one.

How does one measure their value and worth in life?
It's by how much a person gives and shares with the world,
not how much a person claims ownership to.

Open your mind and view yourself from within.
It is here that you will find truth and the gates to the path of change.
You need only the courage to walk through it.

The only limits in life are the
limitations we give ourselves.
Just believe.

All humans are truly free, for no man can enslave
the heart and soul of another.

To truly live and learn from life
do not hold back, follow your heart,
and embrace everything life offers you.

To become whole and find one's center, you must bring
MIND, BODY, and SPIRIT together as one in harmony.

To understand the flow of energy and life, simply observe life
that surrounds you in this physical world.

In nature lies the teaching of the flow of life and energy,
with it's action, reaction, and how life adapts.

Pause for a moment in the elements of life. Observe the movement
of nature around you and feel the flow.

Crying cleanses the soul by allowing the
waterfall of emotions to run free.

Free the mind.

Do not allow your mind to become trapped
in an abyss of negative thoughts and emotion.
Let go of the negative energy and set your mind and soul free.

You must first learn to love yourself
before you can truly love others and life itself.

Fear can never hurt you
for you control your own fear.

Learn to redirect this energy to keep a clear mind,
focus on the moment, and you can overcome any challenge.

Always have hope.

It's easy to look the other way
but if you let go of hope you feel lost in life.
Realized or not, you're still on your path in life
so hold onto hope and have faith.
The greater the challenges you face in life
the more you learn for the soul's great journey.
Always have hope.

Inspire yourself by putting compassion, pride, and joy into your duties and actions in life, and you shall find fulfillment.

Before a person can hear the answers to the questions of life, one must first learn how to listen.

To inspire another to do right,
you must first start with yourself.

Every journey, large or small, starts with a single step.

Let go of your fear and doubts of the journey and take the first step, and you will find your path one step at a time.

The only untrustworthy person
is a person you are not willing to trust.

Many human reactions are done defensively and in fear.
Lay down your burden of fear and embrace the moment
with compassion and clarity of mind,
and you shall overcome the limitations from fear
and see the truths of life.

Our only true enemy is ourselves.

The mind is like a window,
the more you clean it
the better you can see beyond it.

Happiness is not a cause, it's a choice.

When it rains one must decide to stay inside and hide or dance in the rain, but it's up to you to choose.

When one can quiet the storms of the mind
one can feel the energy of life.

Knowing who you are should come from within
and not from others.

Life is about choices.
Within each new day the sun brings light.
You must choose if you see the light or only the shadows.

The body's abilities are only limited to
the imagination of the mind.

Every element of the body is alive and ever changing,
acting and reacting with time, life, and the challenges endured.

Like the branches of a tree, a person can strengthen the bones
by exercising with impact, which causes the energy of the bones
to rebalance it's density where it's needed.

One who achieves stillness and peace of mind
gains great control over the body.
Including one's own flow of energy and life force.

To pray is to speak to God,
to meditate is to listen.

The path to enlightenment
is between both ways of extremes.

He who takes time to put pride in his tasks in life
finds fulfillment in life.

Life cannot be taught,
it must be lived to be understood.

Find the courage and compassion to walk your path
and thus finding the meaning of life.

To rule is to command
to lead is to inspire.

The key to life is to live life as a lesson of love and NOT a battle to survive. Otherwise you lose the meaning in the fight and life itself.

Sometimes to find yourself,
you must first lose yourself.

Life is not about the destination
it's about the journey.

Life is not about simplicity and luxury of the life you live,
it's about the challenges and hardships.
Without it, what would we learn from?

Thoughts are things.
Always be mindful of your thoughts
for one's energy follows with one's thoughts.

One does not have to cause a great impact to start change, because even the largest of objects, needs only a starting point.

If you want to understand life then you must first learn to listen. Not with your ears but with your mind, body, and spirit.

To master this is to truly hear life with the heart and soul.

With every battle won, courage is born.
With every battle lost, understanding, strength, and determination are born.

The journey we live each day is really the destination because the destination is the journey.

Anything is possible.
Just open your mind to the possibility and believe.

Time does not truly exist.
It's merely a measurement of movement
from only one location and perspective.

It's from this one point in question
that it has bearing to it's surroundings.

Energy is in everything and is ever flowing.
When you understand this, you can learn to help direct this flow.
Everything we do and think effects this flow like ripples in a pond.
Learn to put your conciece mind behind these ripples, directing the
flow for what is truly important in your life.

Sometimes we must face the darkness
to see the light.

Mind over matter.
You create your own limitations from within
by your own point of view.
If you think it cannot be done then
you're creating your own obstacles.
You must first believe in yourself and that anything is possible.

Thoughts are things.
Your vision of yourself becomes reality of who you are
and who you become.
Like a flowing river, steer yourself to what you want,
not what you don't want.

When you look for the understanding of life,
the truth shall find you.

You cannot fight fire with fire,
instead fight fire with water.
Just like you can't fight anger with anger,
it will only lead to a greater fight.
Instead fight with love and you will always win
no matter what the outcome.

If you want to learn how to stand strong,
you must first learn to fall.
If you want to learn to succeed,
you must first learn to fail.

A smart man learns from his mistakes.
A wise man learns from others.

Life is like a set of stairs.
You either see it as a stack of obstacles, one after the other,
or steps to help you get where you need to go.

Reality is what you choose to see.

Our actions are the mirror images of our thoughts and feelings.

Life is not a series of to-do's,
it's a series of choices and experiences.

Never attack out of anger.
For even if you win, you loose.

All species of life are happiest when understood
creating harmony for all.

In life each person we encounter is a new teacher.
Together we hold knowledge as vast as the ocean.

Crying releases the trapped emotions of the soul,
laughing can light up the path to happiness.

What happens to one of us
affects all of us.
Always step forward in life
with your heart.

A person can always find a way to overcome a challenge
when they learn to overcome their fears.

Accept who you are and the life you were born into
and you will have greater peace of mind as you take your journey
through your lessons of life.

Never feed into anger, hate, or sorrow.
We must learn to never allow to dim our inner light and always
shine
with positive energy no matter what.

Sometimes our greatest enemy we must face is ourself.

There is a reason why we are all here.
Find the strength and truth in the journey,
and find your purpose in this world and believe.

Do not think in absolutes,
one way is right and the rest is wrong.

It is not about who is right and wrong by difference of perspective.
Instead try and learn from all perspectives.
When you open yourself to be neutral and openminded,
then the world is yours to absorb, understand, and learn from.

In order to change the way you view life
you must first learn to understand and love yourself.
Then you are ready to understand and love all life.

How can you love at all if you do not love yourself?

To hold hate and anger in your heart is to attack yourself.
To forgive is to rise above the challenge
and absorb the lesson at hand.

Do not simply judge a human or animal by it's action
but also by the reason behind the action.

Does a snake attack out of anger, or out of fear when approached?

The teachings of existence and life cannot be shown and explained,
it must be lived to define it's meaning and truly be absorbed.

A human mind is like a storm.
Learn to calm the storm
and you shall find understanding of the deepest of questions.

To stand alone you limit your potential
to stand together, there is no limit to the possibilities of growth.
We must learn from one another, not work against one another.

When you feel you have lost your way
sometimes you need to go back to the beginning
to see the path again.

Those consumed by desire and physical things
live blind to the true riches of life and beauty it brings with it.
Let go of desire and see life through heaven's eyes.

Eyes are but only one way to see life.
View life from within and see the true colors of life.

A blind person can show you a vision beyond
what you can see with your eyes.

The difficulty of making choices is not what you choose, but understanding the meaning of the choice you made.

If you have everything
then you have nothing.
If you have nothing
then you have everything.

One can be taught the lessons of right and wrong
but it is our mistakes that we can truly learn from and grow.

One cannot know pain if they have never experienced it.
One cannot understand sadness without loss.

Sometimes one must look from the outside in
to see the solution.

Build a staircase to your dreams
and you'll reach them one step at a time.

When one can master the stillness of the mind
a mind is truly free.

Teachings give us the reasons,
mistakes gives us the understanding.

You can't fill a cup which is already full.
Empty the cup and taste life.

We cannot truly understand how to succeed
without failure to point the way.

A person's true character is defined
within their challenges they face.

Sometimes the most obvious of answers
are the most difficult to see.

The soul controls the mind.
The mind controls the body.
Control your thoughts and master your life,
for thoughts are things.

The human soul is ever changing and learning,
like an artist reflecting on his own sculpture.
One should always seek understanding from their lessons
in life to learn and evolve.

Through suffering and pain
we learn compassion.

Knowing the truth can be the easy part,
acting on it is the true challenge.

Start each day with an open mind and you'll learn
something new each day.

Trust in yourself,
free your emotions that lie within your heart
and your soul shall be free.

Do not worry or fear life.
Instead accept life,
learn from life,
move forward, and live life.

Devote yourself completely to whatever you do or pursue, and you will find fulfillment no matter what the outcome.

The true journey is the journey within.

Never underestimate yourself and always dream, and dream big.
Don't let others tell you what you're capable of,
the only true limitation in this life is your imagination.

Understanding the power of opposites
is a key to understanding the flow of energy and life itself.

Look for the good in every moment.

Life is not about how it begins or ends
it's about every step you take.

The more you experience, the more you evolve.
For the life you live today
is only a few steps in your overall existence.

Be patient with yourself.
Do not become discouraged from your mistakes and imperfections.
Learn what you can from them and seek the lesson within the
challenges you face and evolve to what you aspire to be.

You can be a leader, a follower, or stand aside.
A wise person knows how to do all three.

Elements in life must be out of balance to create balance.

Movement creates change and change creates movement.

Even the simplest teachings of life can be understood by observing nature around us, like plants and animals.

Home should be a place of peace, happiness, and above all, love.
Offering sanctuary for the soul to find time for
reflection and meaning in life.

To battle your challenges with love,
you hold the most powerful element in life.
With this you do not destroy your enemy, you transform them.
You can transform hatred into forgiveness, anger into happiness,
and evil into good.

You cannot see through water that is not still,
learn to still the mind and see the answers you seek.

When you create or accomplish something,
have the courage to let it go.

The circle of life is an ever changing circle
because destiny encompasses change.

There are no limits in life
except the limits we set in our own mind.

How we view our life defines the kind of life we live.

In life we are all searching for the purpose in life.
But the search of the understanding in things
is the purpose and journey of life.

Live, love, and enjoy all that life brings your way,
and if it must rain, then dance and sing in the rain.

Don't be afraid to fall, otherwise
you'll never learn how to pick yourself up.

Behind every job there is a purpose.
Find the purpose and you will find the meaning.

Find love in everything you do
and every breath you take.

Understanding and wisdom
comes only at the speed that one can accept.

Humor is an unlimited source of strength,
keep a sense of humor when facing life, including yourself.

Know that nothing stays the same
everything is ever changing.

Life is an adventure,
don't just survive it, live it.

Some of the most beautiful things in life
are the emotions we feel in our heart.

Always seek understanding in every moment
and you will find meaning in every challenge and lesson in life.

True strength does not come from physical ability
but from will power and determination from the heart.

Rise or fall, it's a choice.
The day is what you make of it, not what happens in it.

To succeed in life it's not about the resources,
it's about the resourcefulness of the person.

In life we must be like water, willing to bend and flow as needed to
conform to the world around us, and move in harmony to
overcome our challenges.

You cannot fill a cup that is already full.

If one truly seeks understanding
you must first empty your cup.

Hitting a breaking point in one's life
is an opportunity for a breakthrough.

Look at a problem as a door of opportunity,
you only need to walk through it.

Always love yourself, life,
and all that is in it.

We all fall down in life
but how we get up defines who we are.

When you become lost in struggles, and the what if's in life,
you only need to remember two things:
don't forget to breathe and believe,
and you'll find your way.

One of the greatest secrets in life is there are no limitations to life
except the ones you place on yourself.
Free your mind and live the life you choose.

You can only move forward if you're reaching forward.

To hear one another
we must first learn to empty our thoughts and opinions.
Only then can we truly understand one another.

If you can find inner peace you will see the world transform
around you and become more beautiful than words can describe,
because your mind will open up like the sky to bare all it's beauty
even in it's darkest corners.

What would life be like without challenges?

What is more destructive in life?
Gain or loss,
to have or not to have?

Always remember the past
to be successful in the future.

Life isn't about finding yourself,
it's about creating yourself.

The reason behind the action
is more important than the action itself.

Always have a purpose for one's actions.

Insight is everything.
We live our lives in this world by how we see it.
Change your view from within
and change the world.

See the joy in every moment life brings and express your happiness with smiles and laughter, and the world will follow.

To know your neighbor is to embrace your neighbor.

Be mindful of every positive and negative thought
you aim at yourself,
as it will resonate in your soul.

Be a voice of inspiration for change.

One last quote to live by that stands out as 3 principals to always be mindful of to help keep a person in balance in life with stress, challenges, and our overall daily lives.

3 Things You Should Always Be Mindful Of:

1. Live in the Moment
Always focus your energy at the task at hand becoming one with the moment, and your mind, body, and spirit as one.

2. Have Faith
Trust in yourself and in God. Seek understanding in your challenges in life, because there is meaning behind everything.

3. Breathe
Do not allow yourself to become lost in negative thoughts like frustration, anger, doubt, and sorrow. Take a moment of pause and breathe. Breathe in and out and allow the mind and heart to clear and focus.

Thank You

I hope this book has offered you not only inspiration, but has empowered you with the tools and action steps to take charge of your life, goals, dreams, and desires in life.

"Life is not about finding yourself, it's about creating yourself. Build a staircase to your dreams and you'll reach them one step at a time." –Daniel Skarie

For more inspirational articles, stories, and inspiring quotes, please visit us at www.signstoinspire.com.

www.ingramcontent.com/pod-product-compliance
Lightning Source LLC
Chambersburg PA
CBHW020736180526
45163CB00001B/255